a new look at
KNITTING

a new look at
KNITTING
...An Easier and More Creative Approach

by ELYSE and MIKE SOMMER

text and designs, Elyse Sommer
photography, Mike Sommer

CROWN PUBLISHERS, INC., NEW YORK

WITHDRAWN

Designed by Laurie Zuckerman

LIBRARY OF CONGRESS CATALOGING IN PUBLICATION DATA
Sommer, Elyse.
  A new look at knitting.
  Bibliography: p.
  Includes index.
    1. Knitting. I. Sommer, Mike, joint author.
II. Title.
TT820.S63 1977   746.4'32   77-7121
ISBN 0-517-52860-6
ISBN 0-517-52861-4 pbk.

Contents

Acknowledgments

Gathering contributions and working out designs for this book has been an exhilarating experience. Thank you hardly suffices for all who sent photographs or lent their work for our camera.

Beyond providing actual samples, fellow knitters were incredibly generous in sharing their methods and discussing their views toward their work in particular and knitting in general.

In presenting new techniques it is important to test them out with experienced craftspeople, and in this department extraordinary thanks go to Sara Lane, Nancy Lipe, and Hanna Wildenberg. Since Sara and Hanna are New Yorkers it was possible to develop projects via personal brainstorming. The three thousand miles separating us from Nancy and Dewey Lipe in Palo Alto, California, proved an easily surmountable barrier. Nancy's enthusiastic and active response to scribbled "previews" and bits of samples of things like the knitted ruffle served as the needed impetus to continued experimentation. All these "test pilots" spent long hours sampling ideas offered at this end, and always adding something extra of their own.

When Dori Graepel, whom we knew as a "classic" knitter, wrote that she was planning to set aside her knitting needles for a while in order to delve into the mysteries of batik and textile printing, she seemed the perfect person to query regarding the possibility of printing onto a knitted surface, a different sort of tapestry or color knitting. Dori responded with a group of very handsome painted and printed knits that should start readers off on all kinds of new ideas.

Without Linda Mendelson the chapter on machine or loom knitting would not have been possible and Susanna Lewis's extraordinary work in that medium more than confirmed our judgment about giving coverage to the loom.

We are most grateful to Bob Pomeranz of the Cascade Fiber Company, and Paul Cleaver and Ed Gutowski of Folklorico Yarns for supplying us with some of the materials used for samples and demonstrations.

Thank you to Abe Ginsberg of Ace Camera in Lawrence, Long Island, for so carefully and efficiently processing photos, and to Brandt Aymar for continuing to be the answer to every author's dream, an editor who always cares. Last but not least, appreciation is due our daughter Joellen for being ever helpful as a model and doer of chores that would otherwise be left undone.

Elyse and Mike Sommer,
Woodmere, Long Island, New York
1977

Foreword

The ideas and methods presented in these pages are not intended to replace the beautiful old patterns and delicate, dainty textures found in traditional knitting. Instead, *A New Look at Knitting* represents yet another chapter in the ongoing history of a craft that traces its origins to antiquity.

A New Look at Knitting, like *A New Look at Crochet,* was born out of the belief that modern design and technique innovations warranted special documentation, alongside the historic pattern books. Experimentation in knitting has not yet enjoyed quite the momentum of crochet. The mystique that surrounds knitting as a difficult and demanding craft has been reinforced by the many intimidatingly long and involved published patterns, as well as a certain rigidity that has marked most knitting instruction. Perhaps, too, knitting's *super*-utilitarian appeal—few garments are more comfortable than knitted ones—has obliterated anything but the obvious and accepted applications.

Knitting has a marvelously resilient quality. It is easy to learn, requires few tools, and has great portability. The techniques and ideas offered here were designed to make it even easier and more portable, and most importantly, to stimulate originality and inventiveness rather than slavish adherence to patterns and standard projects.

The organization of text and illustrations was planned to immediately involve both the novice and the experienced knitter. The expert will find novelty skills even in the early chapters. Sample projects are grouped according to how they best fit in with the methods being discussed and taught, not according to object categories. Construction information, like technique directions, is provided to encourage understanding, and not necessarily to be copied.

Garments have been developed in the spontaneous fashion introduced in *A New Look at Crochet.* Most are knitted from the center out rather than the usual bottom-to-top method which permits little alteration in either fit or design plan. Paper patterns or sample garments are used as size and shape guides, eliminating much tedious counting of stitches and rows. There are some beautiful patterns appearing in needlework magazines, and the present approach will be helpful for a better comprehension of patterns and the making of changes to suit individual preference.

Unlike chapters 2 through 9, which will be most profitably read with knitting needles and yarn at hand, chapter 10 is less likely to be a work-along experience. Thousands of knitting machines have been sold, and advertisements for various brands are in evidence in many needlework magazines; yet nothing has been published to guide and inspire those who are curious about the artistic potential of these ingenious devices. Chapter 10 is a first move in this direction.

Knitting is one of the great dual crafts, firmly entrenched in the realm of needlework, with an equally solid footing in the ever-expanding area known as fiber art. Whichever level of involvement you choose, we hope you will gain as much pleasure and satisfaction from this book as we did in putting it together. As already stated, knitting represents an additional chapter in an ongoing story. The next chapter will be written, or knitted, by all of you.

South American Knitted Doll with Babies. Collection of the authors.

1
Knitting: Yesterday, Today, and Tomorrow

The craftsperson who breaks new ground with methods and materials used and forms created often needs to step back into the past to better navigate the forward moves. The ground being broken by contemporary knitters is more a fresh interpretation than a rejection of traditional stitches. The newness lies in the way the stitches are handled, the textures and colors used, and the results obtained.

The most adventurous knitters are often the most avid students and collectors of historic specimens, for they fully appreciate the debt they owe to all those who have laid the groundwork for the current wave of creativity and experimentation.

Freeing yourself from the stitch-by-stitch, row-by-row copy approach to knitting will be easier if you have an understanding if not a working knowledge of the intricacies as well as the basics. An awareness of the integral and important role of knitting in the history of textiles will provide that added impetus, pride in being involved in a craft that has demonstrated sufficient challenging power to sustain interest, pleasure, and appreciation since A.D. 200. With this in mind, let's start our NEW LOOK at knitting with a brief survey of where and how it all began.

Yesterday

Probably only toolmaking precedes fabric construction in the annals of human progress. The perishable nature of fabrics, and the early historians' failure to specifically identify the techniques of ancient textile fragments, makes some stories of early knitting more legendary than factual.

Textiles were described as woven or hand wrought, the latter referring to some form of looping method so that both knitters and crocheters have laid claim to some of these earliest specimens. Mary Thomas in her *Knitting Book* speculates on the possibility that Christ's seamless garment was knitted, that Eve knitted the pattern on the serpent's back, and that Penelope's web might have been the first example of frame knitting. While legends tend to be nurtured on a mixture of truth and embellishment, sufficient numbers of scholars are in agreement on the point of definitely establishing the geographic origins of knitting in Arabia, at about A.D. 200.

The term Arabic knitting has become a generic one covering all the earliest known types of knitting executed by the nomads of the North African desert. The work was done on a frame, similar to the familiar knitting knobby, and the objects thus created were socks, tent flaps, and some garments.

Today's men who are increasingly attracted to the more gentle arts should take courage to cast off the last vestiges of existing prejudice against so-called women's work from the fact that those first nomadic knitters were men, as were the traders and sailors who disseminated knowledge of the craft beyond the Arabian desert. When knitting reached its zenith during the Elizabethan and Tudor periods, it was again men who created the magnificent, multicolored garments and carpets the completion of which was a requirement for memberships in the professional knitting guilds that marked this era. It was only after the invention of the knitting machine that the men left the field wide open to the opposite sex.

The overall story of knitting, by both men and women, has become a truly international one. Knitters from many countries have placed the stamp of their particular heritage upon their designs. James Norbury spent many years in search of examples of these ethnic distinctions and the results are available in an outstandingly informative and scholarly volume entitled *Traditional Knitting Patterns from Scandinavia, the British Isles, France, Italy, and Other European Countries.*

In addition to close links with weaving and embroidery due to the knitters' attempts to simulate woven cloths and embroidered silks and brocade, the craft also played a vital role in the story of lacemaking. By the early eighteenth century the popularity of white linen and cotton embroideries reached fad proportions and it did not take the lacemakers long to recognize the time- and cost-saving advantages of knitted lace. Samplers of different lace patterns, doilies, and counterpanes came into great vogue throughout Europe. In recent years nostalgia buffs and needlework students have assiduously searched out samples of antique lace or white knitting.

THE INTERNATIONAL LANGUAGE OF KNITTING

Linda Mendelson collects ethnic patterns as inspiration for her machine-loom designs. The sock at right is Greek, the glove Turkish.

The pointed hat is from Peru. The origin of the cap is unknown. Collection of Linda Mendelson.

Examples of very fine lace knit edgings, doilies, and counterpane, from the collection of Susanna Lewis.

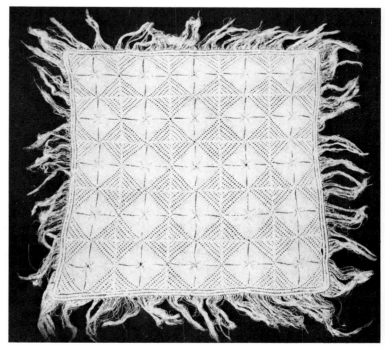

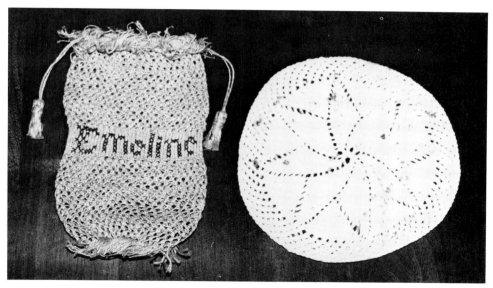

An antique doily and an antique knit purse with name in cross-stitch embroidery on stockinette knitting. Collection of Susanna Lewis.

The Hobby Knitter's Workbasket

The early knitting guilds were obviously commercial enterprises. The apprenticeships took some six years to complete, three of which were spent learning techniques and three traveling, with a final three months devoted to completing a large tapestry carpet, a beret, a shirt, and a pair of socks. Lace knitting also came into full flower as an income-producing activity, and ethnic-motif garments and accessories to this day represent a means of livelihood. Once the knitting machine was invented, enabling mechanized production of the hosiery that was the basis of much commercial knitting, hand knitting became more and more a feminine accomplishment, a hobby craft.

The use of heavier yarns used to fashion more utilitarian objects might well have been accompanied by innovations in styles but few, if any, of these were forthcoming. Mary Thomas, one of the foremost champions and devotees of knitting as a fine art and craft, actually speaks of "the decline of knitting." The emphasis on bulkier utilitarian knitting did *not* end the craftswoman's interest in reproducing lacy knit objects. During the Victorian era there was much knitting of lace insertions, counterpanes, and doilies. A popular magazine of that day, *The Ladies' World,* regularly published a page called Artistic Needlework on which were published readers' own favorite "receipts." In order for these examples to be published, readers were required to send actual samples accompanied by clearly and correctly written directions. Every star, as well as commas and periods for sentences, had to be in proper place. To give readers of this book an idea of the intimidating lengthiness of these patterns the reproduction of a small fragment of Heart's Lace is accompanied by Miss Lizzie E. Gould's instructions.

Instructions for Heart Lace fragment submitted by reader.

FOR THE LADIES' WORLD

HEART LACE

MATERIALS, crochet cotton No. 50, medium-sized steel knitting needles.
Cast on 15 stitches.

1. Slip 1, knit 1, over twice, purl 2 together (over twice before purling makes but 1 loop, as once brings thread in front of needle in position for purling), knit 2, over twice, narrow, over, knit 1, over, knit 1, over twice, narrow, knit 1, over twice, knit 2.

2. Slip 1, knit 2, purl 1, knit 3, purl 6, knit 1, purl 1, knit 2, over twice, purl 2 together, knit 2.

3. Slip 1, knit 1, over twice, purl 2 together, knit 2, over twice, narrow, knit 2, over, knit 1, over, knit 3, over twice, narrow, knit 5.

4. Bind off 2, knit 4, purl 10, knit 1, purl 1, knit 2, fagot (over twice, purl 2 together), knit 2.

5. Knit 2, fagot, knit 2, over twice, narrow, knit 4, over, knit 1, over, knit 5, over twice, narrow, knit 1, over twice, knit 2.

6. Slip 1, knit 2, purl 1, knit 3, purl 14, knit 1, purl 1, knit 2, fagot, knit 2.

7. Slip 1, knit 1, fagot, knit 1, narrow, over twice, knit 3 together (slip 1, narrow and throw slipped stitch over), knit 9, knit 3 together, over twice, narrow, knit 5.

8. Bind off 2, knit 4, purl 12, knit 1, purl 1, knit 2, fagot, knit 2.

9. Slip 1, knit 1, fagot, knit 1, narrow, over twice, knit 3 together, knit 7, knit 3 together, over twice, narrow, knit 1, over twice, knit 2.

10. Slip 1, knit 2, purl 1, knit 3, purl 10, knit 1, purl 1, knit 2, fagot, knit 2.

11. Slip 1, knit 1, fagot, knit 1, narrow, over twice, knit 3 together, knit 5, knit 3 together, over twice, narrow, knit 5.

12. Bind off 2, knit 4, purl 8, knit 1, purl 1, knit 2, fagot, knit 2.

13. Slip 1, knit 1, fagot, knit 1, narrow, over twice, knit 3 together, knit 3, knit 3 together, over twice, narrow, knit 1, fagot, knit 2.

14. Slip 1, knit 2, purl 1, knit 3, purl 6, knit 1, purl 1, knit 2, fagot, knit 2.

15. Slip 1, knit 1, fagot, knit 1, narrow, over twice, knit 3 together, knit 4 together, (narrow, narrow, pull last narrowed stitch over first), then with the left needle, slip second stitch on right needle over last knitted stitch, over twice, narrow, knit 5.

16. Bind off 2, knit 4, purl 2, knit 1, purl 1, knit 2, fagot, knit 2.

Repeat from first row.
LIZZIE E. GOULD.

Heart Lace pattern published in *The Ladies' World,* 1897.

Knitted hosiery once a major handicraft became largely automated with the advent of the first hosiery machine.

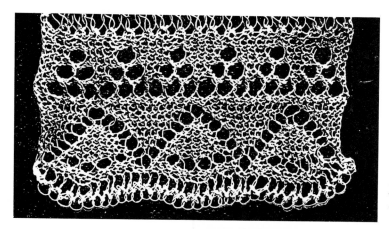

Pyramid Lace Knitting sample, *The Ladies' World,* 1897.

Five years later, in 1902, lace "receipts" were still being exchanged in the pages of *The Ladies' World,* for example, this delicate motif for a handkerchief.

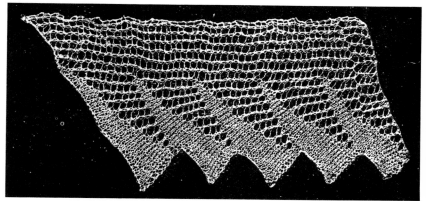

Typical Projects for Yesterday's Knitters

A typical and rather timeless gift, the baby blanket. The use of strips of popcorn stitches alternated with plain knitting does give proof that inspiration for new ideas lies within the traditional examples. (See chapter 9.)

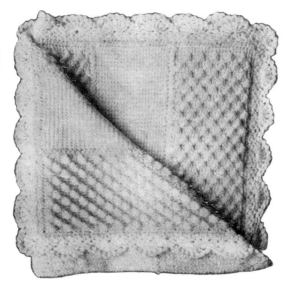

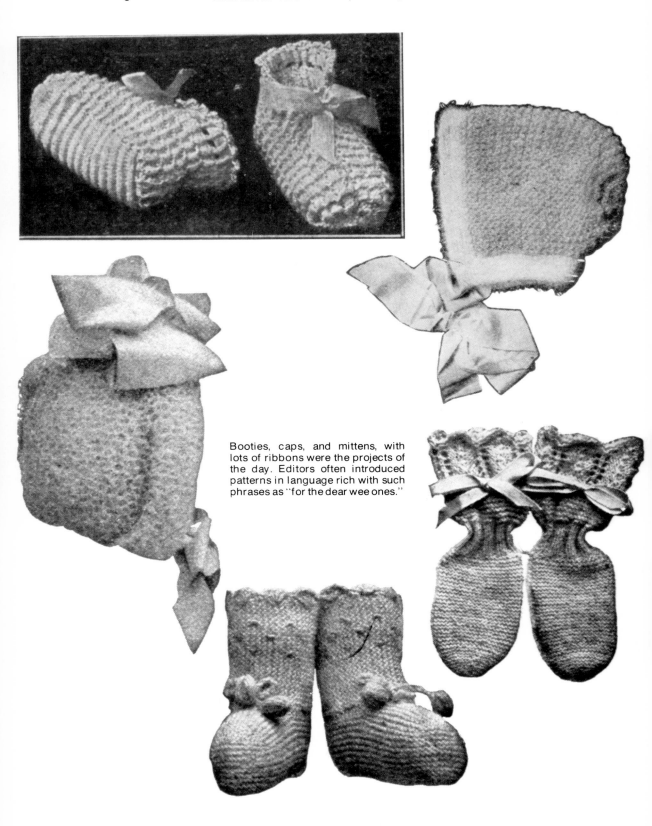

Booties, caps, and mittens, with lots of ribbons were the projects of the day. Editors often introduced patterns in language rich with such phrases as "for the dear wee ones."

Love Victorian Style

In 1906 the editors of *The Ladies' Home Journal* devoted a full page to the making of gifts for the men in readers' lives, gifts that would actually be used, for to quote the editor (known only as Mrs. Grabowskii), "sad to relate, it matters not how much in love a man may be, he will not use or wear most of the many things that women make for him!" According to Mrs. Grabowskii, the secret of gift-giving success lay in articles at once useful and conservative enough to appeal to current tastes.

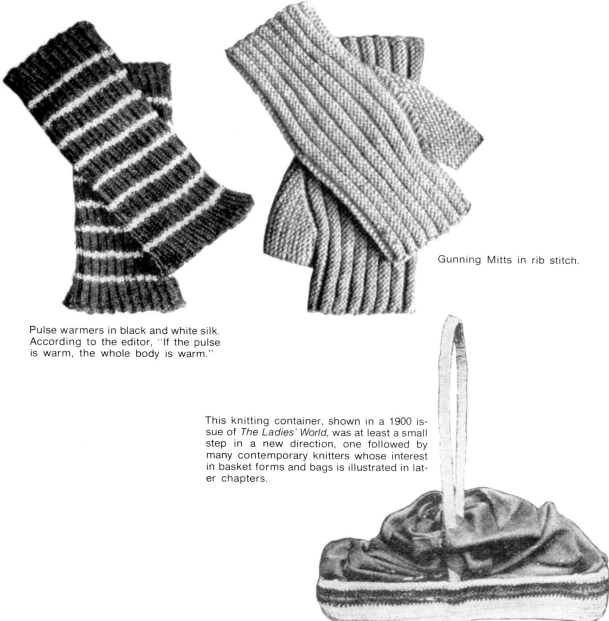

Gunning Mitts in rib stitch.

Pulse warmers in black and white silk. According to the editor, "If the pulse is warm, the whole body is warm."

This knitting container, shown in a 1900 issue of *The Ladies' World,* was at least a small step in a new direction, one followed by many contemporary knitters whose interest in basket forms and bags is illustrated in later chapters.

These silk four-in-hand ties were to be made on four needles, like the pulse warmers and the mitts.

Today and Tomorrow

The years of sameness in the type of knitting being done combined with some of the negative associations that have been allowed to grow up around knitting, have done very little in the way of favorable public relations for the craft. Expressions such as "just woman's work" and "endeavor for the old and feeble," or "stick to your knitting," have become all too familiar. Even politically, knitting suffered from negative rather than affirmative notoriety when during the French Revolution there were widely circulated stories about Parisian women knitting as they viewed the executions, counting the falling heads without losing count of their stitches.

A casual notetaking of current references to and portrayal of those who knit shows vestiges of negative attitudes. Television programs and movies when characterizing dull homebody types often stick boring-looking sweaters or socks-in-progress into the hands of the actress portraying the part. Male knitters tend to be characterized as offbeat, peculiar types. A fellow Crown author who wrote a very fine and contemporary text on a happier and more positive sort of old age gave a newspaper interview in which he implied that older people had the choice of following his good advice or "staying home and knitting."

I feel optimistic that these prejudices will evaporate as more people become aware of knitting as a very contemporary craft, an art form as well as a practical and pleasant pastime. Much knit art is already in evidence, with recognition via gallery and museum exhibits . . . more, much more is in the making.

The fiber arts are constantly merging. Artists are regularly delving into auxiliary media to make their statements. As more and more teachers incorporate knitting into their fiber programs, we will see still more of an influx of knit art. Mary Walker Phillips, often called the foremost knitter in the United States, has taught numerous workshops and her teaching and exhibits have inspired many. Diane Sheehan, a fiber art teacher at Purdue University in Indiana, has only recently ventured into knitting, using her knowledge of weaving to spontaneously work out knitting problems. Her work as well as that of a student, B. Joan Langley, can be seen in the color section and text.

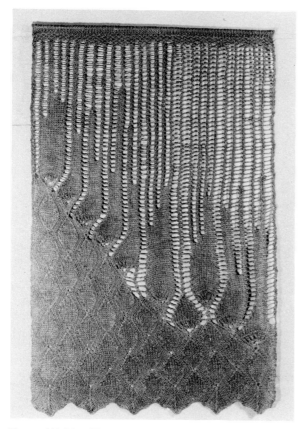

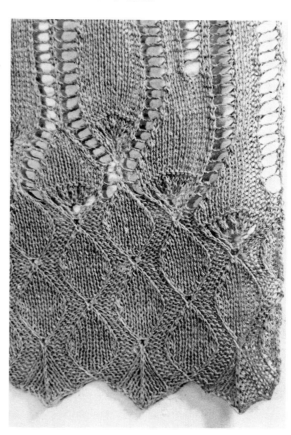

Howard Zabler filled many of his requirements for his art degree at the University of Wisconsin with knitting projects. He also studied independently and made this beautiful linen sampler during a workshop taught by Mary Walker Phillips.

The irregular bottom is the result of Howard's departure from the base pattern, which was taken from *Mary Thomas's Book of Knitting Patterns*.

Howard has also essayed into more fantastic and sculptural directions. This marvelous sheep's head was made to cover a missing piece of a mirror in a friend's yarn shop.

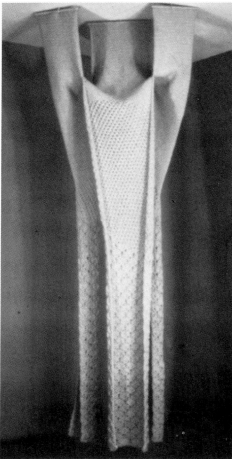

Until an article in *Craft Horizons* changed her mind, Christine King was convinced that knitting was confining and stifling. "I hated doing socks, mittens, and sweaters!" she recalls. Today, knitting is her exclusive technique in fibers. "Tranquility," which measures 2½' by 1½' by 9', was part of the June 1976 Fiber Structures show at Carnegie-Mellon University's Heinz Gallery.

This detail shows how Christine King uses traditional stitch patterns to create forms that represent statements very much rooted in the present. The color section illustrates another knit piece from the Fiber Structures show, "Red Tide," by Deborah Frederick.

The lace doily knitters might recognize their influence on Hermine Secretan's "Serendipity," though there's nothing old-fashioned or rigid about this hoop supported hanging of hand-dyed nylon yarn. The title was suggested by the manner in which the piece developed for the artist. Photo Luc Secretan.

Detail of "Serendipity."

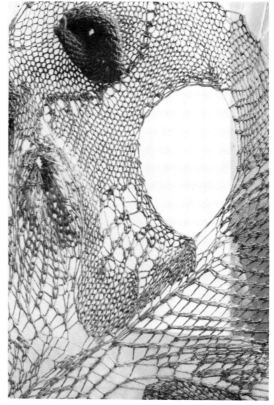

The modern knitter combines a variety of fibers and techniques. Here Jean Legge mixes knitting and stitchery. She calls her hanging "Shore Line."

Until recently knitting machines were used primarily for mass production. However, more and more artists in search of an alternative to weaving discovered the potential of the knitting loom, and the results truly defy the label "commercial." If all who venture into machine knitting bring to it Susanna Lewis's standards of excellence and individuality, loom knitting may indeed be the wave of the future. More on this subject in chapter 9. See color section for another view of this cape.

Nancy and Dewey Lipe combine knitted, crocheted, and fabric tubes into a soft sculpture.

Classically simple sweaters gain a special spark with more fancifully knit appliqués. This sweater was knitted by Nancy Lipe for daughter Miae, photographed by Dewey Lipe. Directions for the ruffles and drawstring balls of the ornament can be found in chapters 2 and 3.

Another classic sweater, done in tapestry or stranded color knitting, with a motif that is a far cry from yesterday's patterns. It was designed and knitted by Dione King for Ed Strait who is, as you may have guessed, in the music business. Photo by Allan Tannenbaum.

2

Getting Started: Materials and Tools, Basic Stitches, and Techniques, Plus Indispensable Auxiliary Crafts

Getting started as a knitter requires little more than a trip to the local yarn or variety store. A whole wardrobe of needles can be gathered for a minimal investment. As for yarns, although learning to choose and use the right yarn to get the desired results is very much part of becoming a creative knitter, the beginner will find that even the least expensive rug yarns are today available in enough colors and textures to make even the humblest projects attractive. With a little enterprise and ingenuity, household string and twine, plastic wrap, and strips of fabric will offer immediate and inexpensive lessons in the properties and inspirational value of out-of-the-ordinary materials.

Needles are available in aluminum, plastic, and metal. They can be easily fashioned out of wooden dowels. Needle sizes range from superfine to broomstick thick. Low numbers indicate thin needles; high numbers, fatter sizes. Few contemporary knitters have need for anything smaller than a #3. Needles are sold in sets of two, with points at one end and knobs at the other; in sets of four with points on each end and in flexible form. The knob-ended needles are designed for straight knitting and the others for working in the round, as for tubular forms. Don't be bound by such rules, however. The patch strip technique discussed later on makes it possible to work large projects and shapes without ever having more stitches than could comfortably fit onto a double-pointed needle without slipping off. I've found these my own favorites for all projects and hardly ever use "conventional" straight

16

needles. When making garments or experimental hangings, working with very few stitches at a time allows the fabric to be free for trying on and trying out rather than being locked into a long needle. The flexible circular needles are useful not only for their intended purpose of working in the round, but for going back and forth. Two or three of these can be used as one giant one, an important consideration when doing large hangings or afghans.

The choice between aluminum, plastic, and wooden needles is one of personal preference, tempered by the type of yarn used and the project at hand. Aluminum needles have the sharpest points and are the most durable. Some people find them a bit slippery and noisy. I like plastic needles for their lightness and smoothness, but not in the circular form where the weight of the aluminum ones seems preferable. Wooden dowel needles are a snap to make, especially if you have an electric sander. Beads or self-hardening clay can be put on the ends. The wood can be made smooth by rubbing with wet and dry sandpaper and very fine steel wool, wetted down. Thin dowels do tend to break, but they're so inexpensive that it doesn't matter. The dowels have the advantage that they can be cut to any length. When not made too smooth, they serve as handy stitch holders. They are very good when working in the round on three or four needles.

As you begin to knit, equip yourself with a sample of each kind of needle, and as you fill out your collection, concentrate on the types you find most useful and comfortable. Do start out at once with at least three or four different sizes, since merely by switching needle sizes while keeping the same yarn you can add interesting texture variations to your work.

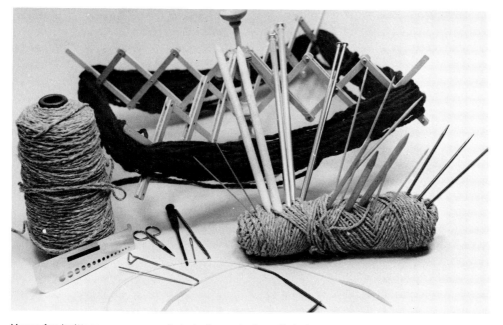

Yarns for knitters come on ready-to-knit spools, in pull skeins or on skeins that must be wound into balls in which case a yarn winder is very handy. Needles are available in wood, metal, and plastic, with knobs at one end, double pointed, or in flexible circular form. You need only a few accessories: a stitch and needle-size gauge, embroidery scissors, one or two crochet hooks, yarn needle, and commercial or improvised stitch holders.

In addition to yarns and knitting needles you will need certain basic accessory tools:

Embroidery scissors to cut thread, a yarn needle, and one or two crochet hooks for joining and decorative purposes. Double-pointed needles and those you make yourself are not marked by numbers so it's handy to have a needle gauge. This is a special ruler with different sized holes, each marked with a number equivalent to a needle size. This handy little gadget also has a second size for measuring work and estimating how many stitches a particular yarn will make per inch. This is known as estimating the stitch gauge. Yarn supply stores also sell special stitch holders to hold stitches not being knit at a particular point of a project. You can also use wooden needles as already suggested, safety pins, or a piece of yarn threaded through the loops.

Optional Tools

Knitting needles as we know them today were preceded by the rake, a frame with pegs around which the yarn is wound two times, with the first wind pulled or looped over the second. The frames used by those first nomadic knitters of the Arabian desert were probably very similar to what most of us have come to know as the knitting knobby or knitting jenny, a wooden spool with four to six nails or brads for winding the yarn, and the center hole used to pull through the finished loops. A number of artists, remembering the horse reins made as children, have applied their adult vision to this childhood toy to create tubes that are in turn woven, plaited, or used as fringes. Diane Itter used a handmade knitting knobby to launch her wonderful "I Freeze, I Burn" (see color section, p. 5). Large rakes or circular needles can be utilized to create weblike space hangings such as "Red Tide" (color section, p. 4) or Linda Hendricks's hanging in chapter 9. For those who find the knitting knobby tedious and slow, chapter 3 offers a very fast and easy way of making closed tubes on two double-pointed needles.

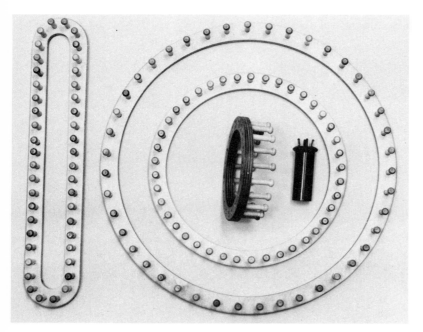

Commercial knitting jenny and a sampling of wooden rakes sold by the J. L. Hammett Company.

Blocking—
Should You, Must You, Can You Do It Yourself?

Most knitting will benefit from some blocking. There are exceptions such as hangings and sculptures supported by armatures or stuffing. Garments should always be blocked before pieces are joined. Blocking before joining is also advised for any patchwork projects.

As for whether or not you can do your own blocking, the answer is, of course you can. It takes a lot more talent to design and knit your own creations than to pin and press them, which is what blocking is all about.

The materials needed for blocking are more than likely a part of your regular household equipment:

A large board (a pressboard is fine) into which pins can be stuck; a large towel or cloth to cover the board; stainless steel t-pins, a ruler, a steam iron, and cotton cloths for the steam pressing.

The procedure for blocking is as follows:

1. Pin your knitting to the cloth-covered board, making sure the t-pins are at an angle, facing outward.
2. Measure your piece to make sure it is the size you want or, as in the case of sleeves, that each sleeve is the same size.
3. Place a damp cloth over the work and press down. *Do not glide* as if you were ironing laundry. The knitting should be thoroughly damp.
4. Allow knitting to dry thoroughly (overnight is fine) before removing from the board.
5. For knitting that has textural stitches or beads or special types of yarn, omit the third step. Instead, spray with water, allow to dry, and remove the pins.

To block, pin knitting to a cloth-covered pressboard. Be sure pinheads are angled toward the outside as shown. Measure and re-pin if necessary. Press with steam iron until thoroughly damp.

Learning to Loop

Both novice knitters and knitting teachers tend to become so involved with how to hold the needles and yarn that they fail to concentrate on what really counts: an awareness of what is happening to the yarn, or how the stitch is actually formed. The continental way of knitting (yarn held in the left hand) *is* faster than the English way and you *will* have to learn to be comfortable with the way you hold your needles and yarn. However, the emphasis on the needles and handhold instead of the action of the yarn tends to prolong the initial awkward stage that accompanies every learning process. Thus, since I am less concerned with correctness of methods than satisfaction with the results, I will not get involved with the right- and left-hand controversy and the many different methods of casting on. The basics illustrated concentrate on the stitches themselves.

The primary principle for the knitter to grasp is that knitting is a looping process. A thread is formed into a loop, passed around the loop and pulled through to form a second loop, thus forming a stitch. Needles are merely implements to ease and expedite the looping process. The chief difference between knitting and crochet is that in the latter each loop is individually locked in by the looping process whereas in knitting as many loops as are required to make the fabric remain open and on the needle.

Howard Zabler feels that the easiest way to overcome the habit of concentrating on the needle and hand action instead of the actual looping is to work with the only tool nature provides, the finger. To prove his point, he demonstrated the basic looping or knitting process for the camera, using his fingers as needles and heavy four-ply jute to prevent the loops from unraveling.

A series of loops are "cast on."

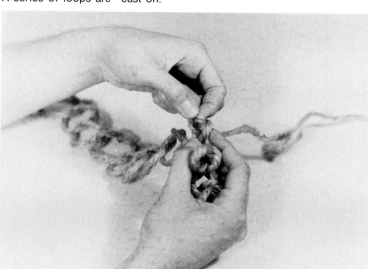

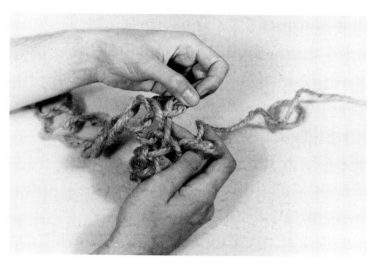

To knit, twist the loop

and pull the yarn through the twisted loop.

Your fingers are the "needle" holding the row of loops.

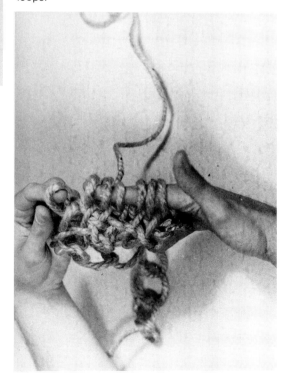

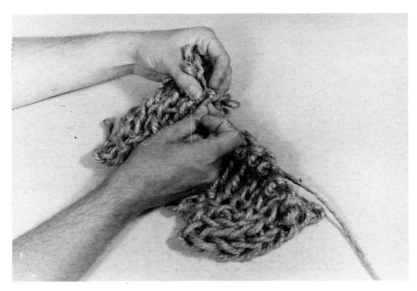

Keep pulling the loops through without turning the work. This will result in one of two basic knitting stitches, the stockinette stitch.

Completed finger-knitted stockinette stitch sample.

Casting Loops onto Needles

Now that you understand the simplicity of knitting, let's free our fingers and get out our needles.

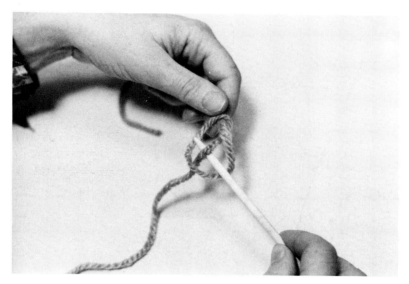

Start with a slipknot.

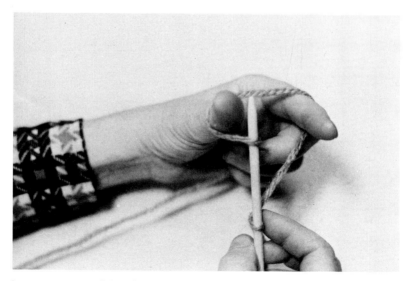

Loop yarn around thumb and forefinger. Insert the needle that has the slip-knot on it *up* through the loop on the thumb and

from the back to the front of the loop on
the forefinger.

Now pull the loop to complete the cast-on.

To once again emphasize the simplicity of how the
stitch is actually made, here is the process illustrated
in the three previous pictures, by hand.

To Knit

Once you master the basic knit stitch, you are on your way to anywhere and anything.

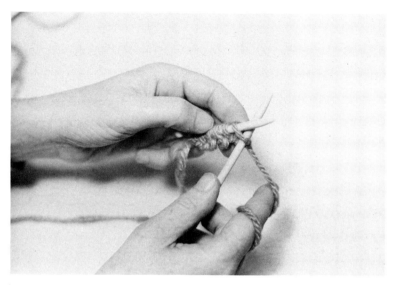

Insert the needle from front to back.

Bring the yarn around from back to front.

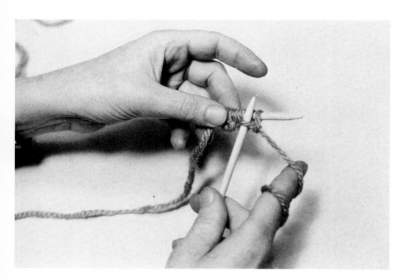

Retract the right-hand needle with the yarn around through the loop on the left needle . . . a back to front, downward motion.

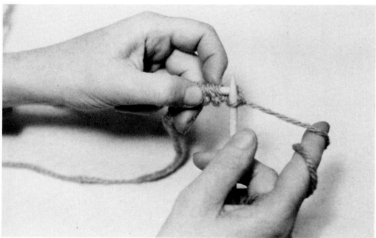

Push the rest of the stitch to the back and off the needle.

If every row is knit, your fabric will look like this and be identified as garter stitch knitting.

To Purl

The chief difference between knitting and purling is that in the latter the yarn is brought to the front of the work. Old-time patterns might refer to the purl stitch as the back stitch, the seam stitch, the ridge stitch, or spell it pearl.

Insert the needle front to back.

Bring the yarn around as shown.

Some people make the knit stitch by going into the back of the stitch (twisted or continental stitch). In that case, purl by throwing the yarn as shown here.

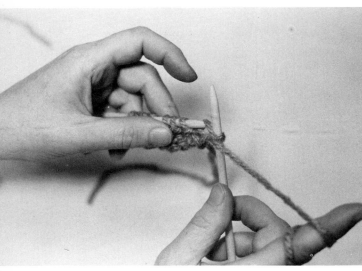

Push to the back and

slip off.

In fabrics where one side is knitted and the other purled, the knit or smooth side is identified as the stockinette side. At top left you see the "regular" stockinette stitch, and to the right, the twisted or continental version. The bottom sample shows the purl or reverse side of the stockinette stitch. Compare it with the garter stitch sample. Many people mistake the two as one and the same, but the purl stitch produces a smaller, finer weave.

Round Knitting

Knitters have several options for knitting round or tubular forms. Flexible circular needles are available in different lengths as well as thicknesses so that one can start with a short needle and switch to a longer one as the work increases. The same kind of knitting can be done by dividing stitches onto three (or four) double-pointed needles. A fourth needle is then used to knit the stitches off the first needle. As the loops are transferred, the needle now freed from the loops becomes the "knitter." This process continues on, or rather, around. Whether you use circular or double-pointed needles, the front side of the work always faces you. The work is not turned so that a stockinette face is formed. Alternatives to knitting from a central circle are presented in chapters 6 and 7.

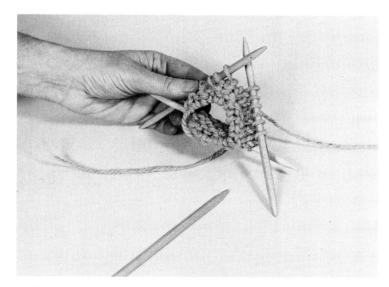

When knitting in the round on double-pointed needles the work is divided onto three out of four needles, with the fourth needle used to knit. This "knitter" needle changes as loops are worked from one needle to another.

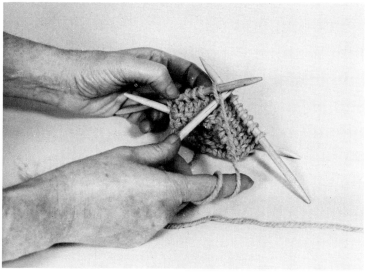

The work is never turned. The front always faces the knitter. Wooden needles that are light and nonslipping are ideal for this method.

Howard Zabler found a pair of superfine lace knitting needles in an antique store. He decided to actually use these to knit a series of eyeballs. The eyeballs started with the pupils, using a single strand of rayon embroidery floss. The rest of the eyeballs are knitted with the floss doubled. The penny shows scale.

The eyeballs begin with four stitches, are increased to forty-eight stitches all around, worked straight for four rows, and then decreased to zero stitches. Each is stuffed tightly with polyester before closing. Howard does some embroidery to simulate the optic nerves.

Basic Skills

Knowing how to increase, decrease, and end off enables you to shape and finish your work. Books that emphasize technique mastery rather than creative results usually document numerous ways of doing this. Herewith the essentials:

To Increase

Increases are most frequently made at the beginning and end of rows. However, the creative knitter will want to experiment. Lots of increases all across a row, followed by decreases in another row, will produce ruffled effects. The outside-in-inside-out square described in chapter 7 is based on increases or decreases made in the middle of the rows.

To increase on knit side, insert the needle into the front of the stitch. Retract, but don't pull off.

Insert needle into the back of the same stitch, yarn over.

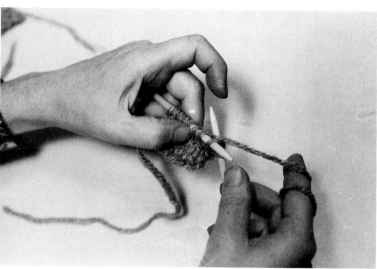

Complete the stitch. You have made two stitches from one. No hole or space will appear in the work.

To increase on the purl side, insert the needle back to front. Yarn over and retract needle. Instead of pulling loop off, insert right-hand needle into front as shown.

Again, you see two stitches made from one.

One of the most important shapes for creative knitting, the triangle can be made by starting at the narrow point (three stitches cast on) and increasing at the beginning and end of each row or every other row (for a longer triangle, i.e., right-hand illustration). You can also start at the widest part of the triangle and develop your shape by decreasing until you get down to three stitches.

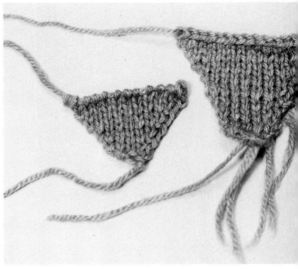

Decreasing and Binding Off

Decreasing is most easily accomplished by knitting or purling two stitches together.

Note: The binding-off method just shown suggests a very useful and frequently used alternative method of decreasing. Instead of knitting stitches together, pass or slip one stitch onto the needle without knitting it. Knit the next stitch and then pull the slipped stitch over the one just knit, just as you did in the binding-off procedure. In knitting jargon, this is abbreviated as PSSO—pass the slipped stitch over.

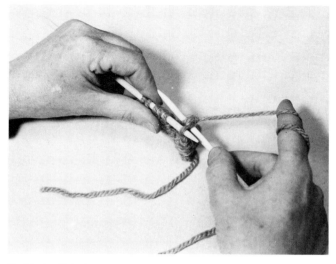

To bind off, knit two stitches and pull the first over the second.

When you get to the last loop, pull through as shown, then cut.

Indispensable Auxiliary Crafts

Crochet and knitting suggest the same everyday associations as apple pie and ice cream, frankfurters and mustard. Patterns for garments are sometimes given in both knitting and crochet, since each craft would be appropriate for the execution. As stated in the introduction, crochet has been embraced somewhat more enthusiastically by artists than knitting, which is more often considered "strictly utilitarian." This book dispels that notion by showing the feasibility of knitting circles and spheres and ruffles and adding on spontaneously. Nevertheless, crochet continues as a vital auxiliary for the knitter in finishing off and joining, in providing contrast interest, or in filling in certain kinds of spaces in large hangings.

Knotless netting is less familiar than crochet, but it has so much to offer that once you become acquainted with it, you may well prefer it where once you might have used crochet. It's so easy to do, if somewhat slower; economical in terms of yarn usage and very compatible with the appearance of knitting. A solid area of knotless netting might easily be mistaken for the purl stitch, though the former lacks the stretchiness of knitting.

Crochet

Crochet, like knitting, is a looping process. A single hooked needle is used rather than two pointed ones. Only one loop remains on the needle at any one time.

As in knitting, casting on starts with a slipknot.

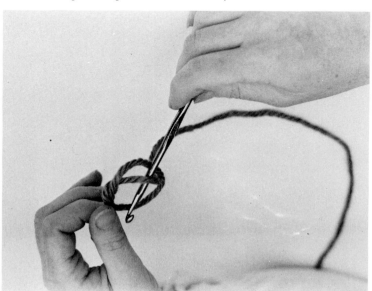

The looping is done by bringing the yarn in front of the loop on the hook and pulling it through to make a new loop. Here you see how to hold the needle, pointing the hook in the direction of the loop for an easy pull-through motion.

The crocheter has only one loop to contend with since each looping motion locks in the previous stitch. By pulling one loop through another a base chain is made.

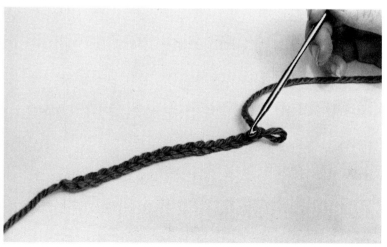

When a chain of the desired length has been made, the hook is inserted into the stitch next to the loop on the needle. In the photo, you see the hook removed, for clarity.

The hook is inserted into the stitch, the yarn brought in front as shown, and pulled through one of the two loops on the hook.

The yarn is brought in front again and pulled through the remaining two stitches to complete the basic crochet stitch, the single crochet.

A new row of crochet always begins with the second stitch, the one next to the loop on the hook. For the knitter, the crochet base is likely to be an edge of knitted stitches or loops.

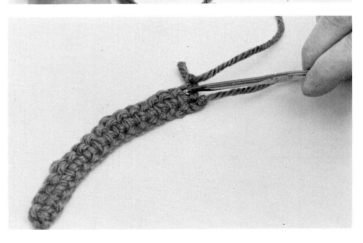

Picking up stitches from an existing surface to create three-dimensional effects was one of the innovations that helped popularize crochet. It's as easy to crochet on top of knitted surfaces as those that have been crocheted. In the next chapter, you will see that you can also knit onto knitting.

New colors can be stranded into the back of crochet work, avoiding any later weaving in. Many crocheters consider this one of the chief advantages of knitting, not realizing that yarns *can* be stranded with equal ease when knitting, as will be seen in chapter 3.

To make a double crochet, bring the yarn in front *before* inserting the needle so that you have three loops on the hook, plus the yarn that will be brought in front.

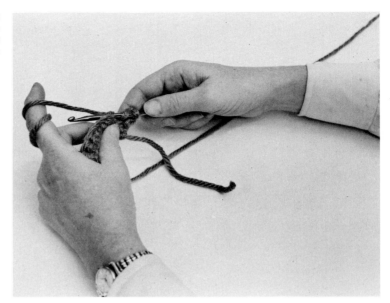

Pull through two loops, yarn over again as shown, and pull through the remaining two loops to complete the stitch.

The Half Double Crochet and the Slip Stitch

The half double crochet is a somewhat shorter version of the double crochet and the slip stitch a shorter version of the single crochet. The half double omits the second step of the double: Bring the yarn around before inserting the hook into the stitch and then loop through all three loops in one movement. The slip stitch employs the same stitch condensation method: The needle is inserted into the stitch and the yarn brought in front as for the single crochet, but the yarn is looped through all in one motion. Slip stitches worked on the surface of a stockinette knit fabric can be used to good advantage by the embroiderer, and a beautiful example of this can be seen in the color section and chapter 11 via Sara Lane's ambitious hanging.

Fancy Stitches in Crochet

Since we have devoted an entire volume to crochet, this chapter confines itself to basic information for the knitter interested in crochet as an auxiliary. For more in-depth information readers are referred to *A New Look at Crochet* as a companion to this book. To give you a sampling of the many pretty crochet accent stitches possible, here's just one particularly knit-worthy fancy stitch, the loop stitch.

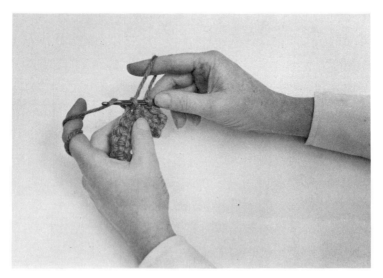

Insert the hook into the stitch and loop around the finger. Hold onto the loop as you complete your stitch and

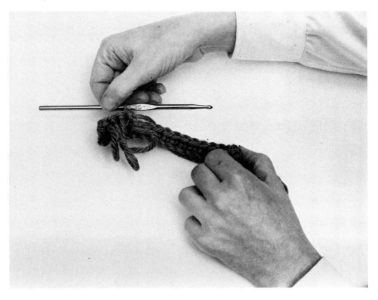

allow the loops to fall toward the back of the crochet work. For loop stitch knitting, see chapter 6.

Knotless Netting

Knotless netting, also a looping technique, is traditionally identified with embroidery and lacemaking. It can be used independently to produce very strong fabrics, or when worked loosely to create open netlike materials. For the knitter this method has a great application as an edging, in joining pieces of knitting, and in creating surface embellishments. The samples are worked on a garter stitch base, but any knit stitch would make a fine base.

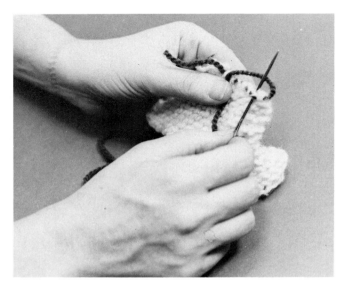

To add a knotless netted edging to knitting, pull your yarn through the edge, using the yarn you pulled through as a base for the loops. The loops, essentially buttonhole stitches, can be worked from right to left

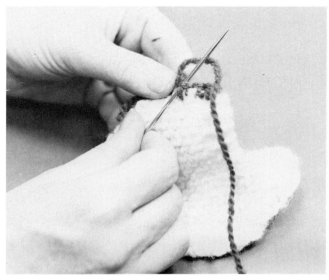

or from left to right. Rows can be worked on top of other rows. Loops can be pulled tight, or gathered very loosely. Increases are possible by inserting the needle several times into one stitch. Conversely, spaces can be created by skipping stitches.

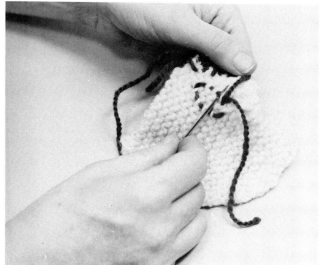

To knotless net on top of a knit surface, use your yarn to create a base for yourself . . . for example, a circle.

As you net or loop around this base, a little cup forms that can be utilized as a decoration or as a case for a stone or other hard object.

3
First Projects and Experiments

In the heyday of lace knitting, people used to make long samplers. As many as a hundred or two hundred patterns would be worked into a roll, like a fat bandage. This was indeed an excellent sort of fiber sketchbook. As a historic reference, a sampler of that type is hard to come by and to be greatly treasured if found. However, in terms of gaining the momentum to really forge ahead and become a creative knitter, there's nothing like making something finished, no matter how small and simple. Sampling *is* important, especially when planning something large, in order to establish the feel for and properties of yarns, and to anticipate problems. Here then are a few learn-by-doing projects, examples of other people's experimentations and ideas to help you dip into your own imaginative resources.

A Basic Skill Project

Try out your basic skills in creating both shape and texture by making an old-fashioned triangular scarf. In Victorian days this type of scarf was known as a fascinator; today it is popular once again among the young and the old. The illustrated triangle is made in stockinette stitch. It starts at the long side with 12 stitches cast on and a single increase made at the beginning of each knit row (in other words, at the right side only). When the triangle is half the desired size, the process is reversed, with a stitch decrease at the beginning of every knit row, until you get back to 12 stitches. Cast off.

To add the ripple effect, an increase is made into every stitch on a knit row, with two stitches purled together (decreased) on the returning row. Alternate these increase-decrease rows with a row of straight stockinette and straight purl (no increasing or decreasing). For a still more pronounced ripple, change needles as you work the increase-decrease and plain rows, using needles about three sizes bigger for the increase-decrease than the plain rows. Edge the scarf with a fringe or a loop stitch. (Crochet loop stitch instructions were given in the previous chapter; knit loop stitch directions can be found in chapter 6.)

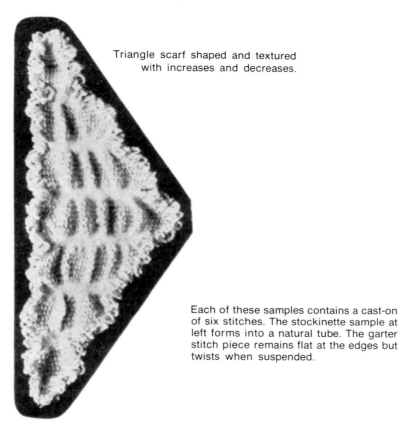

Triangle scarf shaped and textured with increases and decreases.

Each of these samples contains a cast-on of six stitches. The stockinette sample at left forms into a natural tube. The garter stitch piece remains flat at the edges but twists when suspended.

Learn to Make the Most of the Basic Stitch Personality

The stockinette stitch has a natural tendency to curl. Instead of looking upon this as a problem, why not emphasize this characteristic as a plus. Curly stockinette lends itself to all sorts of wonderful tubes and graceful, flowing edges.

The garter stitch while maintaining a flat edge has its own natural bents. Its tendency is to twist when freely suspended but here again this gravity pull can be mobilized as an idea stimulator.

Turn the tubular nature of quickly knit stockinette strips into attractive neckbands to be worn singly or grouped into a colorful choker. The ends are knotted together for an easy soft-button closing. Shiny cotton is used.

The general stretchiness of knitting makes it ideal for garments but something of a problem for some types of art knitting. The stretchiness can be controlled using nonstretchy fibers (knitting worsted probably has *the most* stretch of any type of yarn) and knitting into the back rather than the front of the stitch. One can of course take advantage of the stretch, as Jean Legge did here with "Littoral Drift," which was stretched over a board and then deliberately pulled and twisted to create the waves and pockets that were filled with colorful French knots. The hanging measures 26″ by 40″.

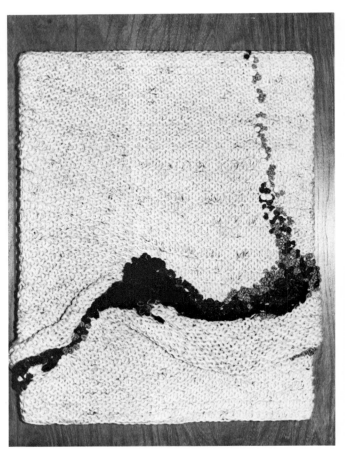

By letting herself go with the natural twist of the garter stitch, Irene Reed created a most effective hanging. The units of this 24-by-17-inch hanging are knitted in a variety of synthetic yarns.

A Box of Stockinette Tubes

Another way to take advantage of the curly nature of the stockinette stitch is to use long tubes as coils. These forms are at once strong and soft, so that they can be worked into combination boxes and pillows. The illustrated sample was made as a container for a good-luck charm that inspired the four-leaf clover shape of the lid and the bright green of the yarns. Only six stitches were cast on, but by stranding three yarns together and using a #15 needle, a very substantial tube resulted. The base tube is 70 inches long, the one for the lid over a hundred inches. When working out something like this it's always best to shape your form before ending off your yarn. When the coils are stitched together, the shape can be further defined.

Cloverleaf box lid with a bit of knotless netting in velour yarn and container with the charm tied to the bottom. In front you see the tube in progress, showing how it forms a natural seam.

Side view of cloverleaf pillow box.

Garter stitch strips lend themselves to a different kind of coiling, like this window hanging by Mary Ann Scarborough. The artist knit together three strands of giant yarn, letting her strips continue for as long as her balls of yarn lasted. She joined and shaped the strips with waxed quilting thread. Photo by Sally Davidson.

Detail photo of garter stitch window hanging.

Christine King experimented with strips of stockinette stitches, in graduated lengths, attached with crochet slip stitches.

A second view of Christine's fiber study illustrates its manipulative potential.

Experiment with Different Fibers

Jute, paper, raffia, plastics . . . try out atypical yarns and see how the nature of the fiber affects the strength and texture and overall appearance of your stitches.

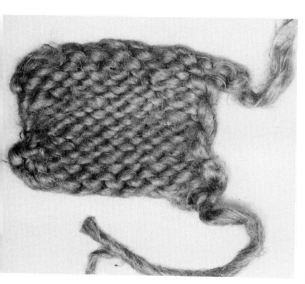

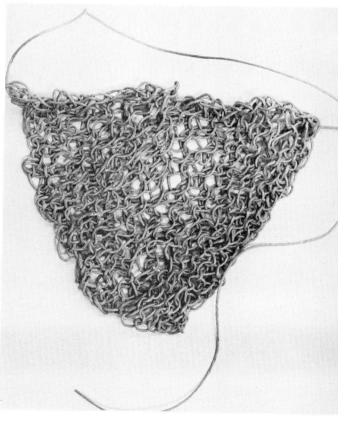

Christine King finds heavy jute a very satisfying material for her large hangings. Here we see the purl side of a sample done in continental or twisted stockinette stitch. The combination of this variation of the basic knit stitch and the jute provides a very solid fabric.

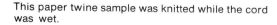

This paper twine sample was knitted while the cord was wet.

B. Joan Langley likes the atypical knit look of raffia and the purl side of the stockinette stitch. The lightness and irregularity and elastic feel of the material seemed to actually guide her investigation into the forms obtainable with increased and decreased stitches. "Navel" started at the outer edge. As the piece decreased, Joan switched from large to smaller circular needles.

The flexibility of the material gives "Navel" a double life as a hanging.

Right: Another increase-decrease shape in raffia, with the purl side of the stockinette stitch facing front.

Left: Close-up view of the untitled form.

The Invisible Cast-on and Cast-off Method for Visibly Original Results

Many knitting manuals don't even get into the invisible cast-on and cast-off method. When I interviewed other knitters, including yarn shop proprietors, I found many were totally unfamiliar with what to me has become not so much an alternative as an exclusive way of working. The method has served as the basis for many other discoveries and its advantages will become more and more evident as we continue onward in this and future chapters.

How does it differ from other methods of casting on and binding off, such as those described in chapter 2? Whereas "conventional" methods create a finished edge, the invisible method gives an open or selvedge-free foundation or finish. To achieve an invisibly cast-on edge, take a length of yarn from the end of your ball or skein and hold it against the needle. This length of yarn should be long enough to stretch through all the loops that will be on your needle (I like to have plenty of yarn to spare). The loops to be knitted are wrapped or woven around the yarn and the needle. To bind or cast off stitches invisibly, the end of the yarn is threaded onto an embroidery needle and drawn through the stitches.

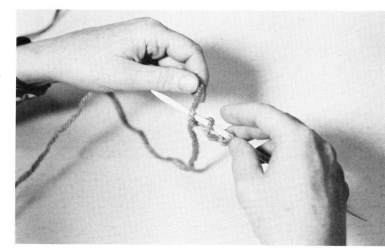

To cast on invisibly, hold a length of yarn along the underside of the needle and wrap the loops around needle and yarn.

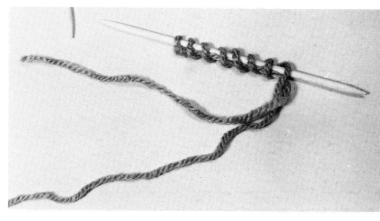

Here you see the loops as they look, wrapped around the base or invisible cast-on yarn.

To cast off, thread the end of the yarn into an embroidery needle. Slip the loops off the needle as the yarn passes through. Don't pull the yarn through too tightly to maintain an even tension and in case you want to remove it at a later point.

Invisible Casting On and Off in Action

The carrot beanbag was shaped by pulling the cast on and off threads tight, drawstring fashion. The end of the drawstring was then used to seam the side with a weaving stitch.

The carrot starts as a stockinette stitch triangle with an invisible cast-on of six stitches. A stitch is increased at the beginning and end of each knit row until there are thirty stitches on the needle. Note the cast-on-off base yarn.

When the cast-on-off yarn is pulled tight, the carrot shape emerges. The drawstring ends are threaded into a yarn needle and the carrot is seamed with a weaving stitch made by inserting the needle down through the center of the first stitch on the right edge, under two rows and through to the right side. It is then passed over and through the corresponding stitch at the left, back under two rows, and so forth. Stuffing is inserted before you get to the end of the seam.

The illustrated beanbag has a plain green fringe to suggest the carrot leaves. You might want to hold up on this decorative finish and substitute some of the little ruffled leaves you will learn to make in the next chapter. The beanbag could also grow into a pillow, by increasing its base size.

A Weatherproof Christmas Wreath

This wreath grew out of some knitting experimentation with Du Pont's craft yarn netting. Forty-eight stitches (use more for a larger wreath) were invisibly cast onto a #15 circular needle, and after just a few rows the knitting curled into a tube so that the purl side became the facing side. The invisible cast-on-off method helped in shaping the circle. The first and last rows were joined by weaving the end of the netting through the top and bottom loops. Copper plastic cord was used to add a decorative design of single crochet stitches on top of the knitted surface.

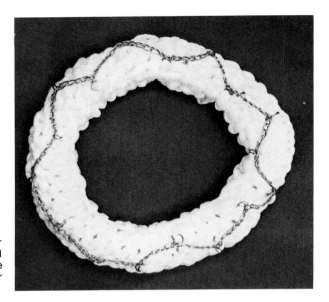

Wreath knitted on #15 circular needle with Du Pont's crystal white craft netting. The crochet trim is plastic copper cord.

Drawstring-Bottom Container

Sue Dauer creates beautifully crafted containers using straight pieces of knitting so that she can line her knitted fabric before forming the final basket shape. Her linings are always color coordinated with her yarns, which are mostly hand spun and dyed. An invisible cast-on enables Sue to tighten the bottom of her containers into solid circular forms.

Knitted container by Sue Dauer. The artist switches from thin to thick needles to create variation in the size of her stitches. Top and bottom edges are in stockinette stitch, the rest is all garter stitch. (See color section, pp. 3, 8.)

The stockinette stitched drawstring bottom is pushed in so that the container rests securely on a tight garter stitch edge.

Diagram showing construction of the container. The A sections are in stockinette stitch. The B sections are garter stitches on thin needles; the C section, garter stitch on fatter needles. The dotted lines at the bottom A section indicate the drawstring shaping. The top A section is folded and stitched to the inside lining. After the fabric is lined, the container is seamed at the zigzagged edges.

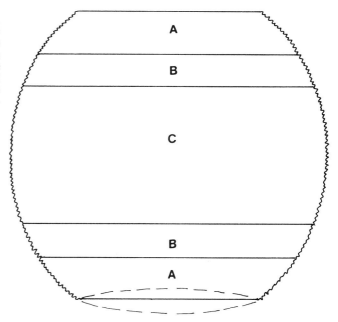

A Knit-Woven Basket

Here's still another kind of knitted container. It's constructed of six straight garter stitch bands, each about 1 inch wide (6 stitches in a tweedy rug yarn). The bands are crisscrossed at the bottom, with two more strips woven over and under the bands extending from the bottom to form the sides. The invisible cast-on-off method is helpful in this case in terms of securely and easily joining the ends of the bands without sewing.

Paper strips serve as models for planning the construction of the basket. Four crisscrossed strips with the sides folded up and sewn together would suffice. However, the additional two bands woven over and under the side bands provide a double layer throughout and make for a sturdier structure.

The crisscrossed knit bands hold quite firmly though you will probably want to use the end yarns to do a little tacking down here and there. The beginning and end of each of the woven side bands were joined by slipping the invisible cast-on-off loops onto a separate double-pointed needle, alternating one from the other and ending off by pulling the yarn through all stitches, then weaving in and out for extra security. This alternate loop-joining method is further illustrated in the section on double knitting in chapter 5 and the examples for joining shapes in chapter 7.

To join the bands at the top edge, knit together the loops from each band as one; or knit a stitch from the front band and one from the back band and then bind off one stitch.

Feathers that are very much a part of basketry are knitted into the edge of the basket. This is done by wrapping the feather in with the yarn as it is brought around the needle. The feathers can also be sewn or crocheted in place.

Drawstring Balls

The invisible cast-on-off serves as the basis of little or big drawstring balls the infinite applications of which have been so generously explored by Nancy Lipe that we often refer to them as Nancy's baubles. The basic formula can be enlarged, knitted in garter, stockinette, or a combination of stitches:

1. Invisibly cast on 14 stitches.
2. Knit 5 rows and cast off invisibly.
3. Pull cast-on and cast-off yarn tight and use ends to seam the side.

To enlarge the formula, increase the 14 stitches to 21, and knit 7 instead of 9 rows; to enlarge still more, use 28 stitches and knit 9 rows, and so on. The balls can be stuffed before closing the side seam.

What can you do with these quick and easy-to-make little knit balls? You'll see many examples and ideas throughout the book. To start, here are five finger puppets all started with a drawstring-ball head stuffed with polyester. The bodies consist of knit pieces, either straight or shaped with increases and decreases, and sewn together. All are designed and knitted by Nancy Lipe, photographed by Dewey Lipe. Five-year-old Miae Lipe is the happy owner.

Fourteen stitches are cast on invisibly. Five rows are knitted; the yarn is threaded into a needle and pulled through the loops,

and drawn together. *Voila*, the ball!

Different sized yarns and needles create different sized balls. The white ball appliquéd to the knit rectangle is a "half recipe" of just three rows. Nancy Lipe likes to use these half balls as little cups in which the full ones can sit.

The buttons on this perky rabbit's jacket are tiny knitted versions of his head. It's all white except for the coral jacket.

This sporty skier's sweater is knitted in two shades of green. His hat is all white. He has sparkling button eyes and a bead nose.

Sunbonnet Sue is all knit. Her arms were made on four double-pointed needles.

Santa's beard and costume trim are in fluffy
angora. His coat and hat are of course bright red.

Another all-knit puppet. The stockinette stitch curls
naturally into the angel's halo, wings, and dress.

4

More Skills for Your Stitches

The facility for changing yarns at random, working in loose ends as one goes along instead of having to neaten things up later, is repeatedly cited as an advantage of crochet over knitting. The reason for this misconception is that the technique for stranding yarns in knitting is usually described only as part of instructions for tapestry color knitting and not for simple yarn changes. Yet this is a vital skill for the knitter since sections of knitting are often left on a spare needle to be picked up later, and it is understandable that the prospect of finishing off all these loose ends would be discouraging. The simplicity of stranding in new yarns as you knit will do wonders in the way it frees you to become more casual about color changes and breaking up solid areas of knitting by working sections in different stitches and directions. The whole concept of knitting on, another idea thought by many to be limited to crochet, grew from an understanding of the advantages inherent in stranding.

Changing and Stranding Yarns

The following demonstration is for switching colors or adding in new yarn when the old runs out. If you were carrying the color as for a tapestry design, you do not cut the yarn.

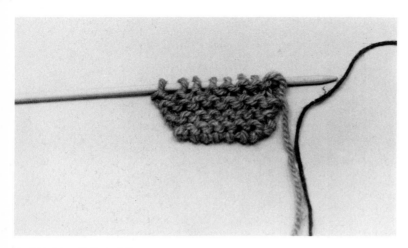

Leave a 6″-to-10″ length of the old yarn and lay in new yarn to match this length.

Bring the new yarn around the needle and knit up to make the first new color stitch.

To start the stranding or weaving-in process, lay the old and new yarns across the needle as shown.

As you complete your second stitch, the stranded yarns fall to the back. They will not show up at the front of the work.

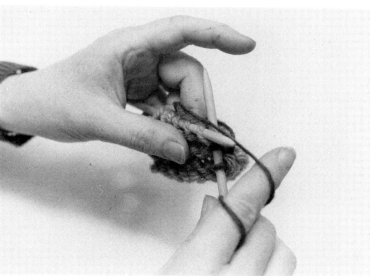

For the next stitch (stitch #3 of the row), do *not* bring the stranded yarn around but let it lay underneath the needle. You can hold it in place as shown. The stitch now made will lock the yarn into place.

Repeat the procedures for stitches two and three. The back of your work will show a woven pattern.

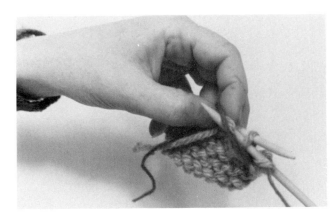

To strand on a purl row, the process is the same, except that the stranding is done at the front, facing the knitter.
IF YOU CHANGE COLORS WITHIN A ROW, AS IN A TAPESTRY DESIGN, <u>BE SURE TO CROSS THE YARNS</u> TO LOCK THE STITCHES TOGETHER AND AVOID A HOLE.

Designing with Stranded Colors

Once you know how to strand in new colors, you can create stripes, free-form designs, or graph out patterns as in needlepoint. Any cross-stitch design is translatable into color knitting. However, though stranding in yarns when *switching* colors is an easy and simple procedure, carrying colors along continuously, changing from one to the other to create a tapestry, does require the interlocking or crossing of the yarns every time there is a color change, so it is best to keep things simple, at least at the beginning. The knitting-on process described later in this chapter and as part of the patchwork procedures in chapters 6, 7, and 8 offers a completely different way of color designing.

Diane Sheehan undertook knitting without any instruction, bringing to the craft her knowledge of weaving and other fiber techniques, as well as an artist's appreciation of color gradations and surface design. Her "I Freeze, I Burn" was an inspired improvisation. Its true beauty can be appreciated by turning to the color section.

"I Freeze, I Burn" began with multi-colored fringes made on a homemade knitting jenny (a spool with six equally spaced brads). The ends of the hand-spun yarn were allowed to spill out from the spool-knitted tubes and were worked into the flat knitted area to continue the colors.

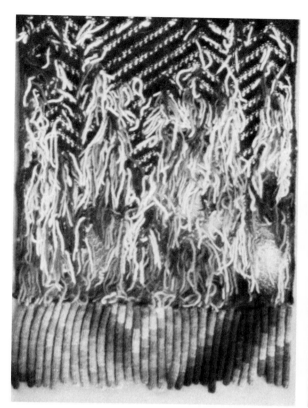

Diane was unfamiliar with color stranding, but she instinctively crossed her yarns as she switched, since she knew as a weaver that stitches need to be interlocked to avoid holes.

Since she did not weave in her beginning and end yarns, Diane allowed them to hang down as a loose pile, and in this instance the richness of the fibers effected a very tactile and colorful rear view.

"I Freeze, I Burn" measures 15" by 21". Photo courtesy artist.

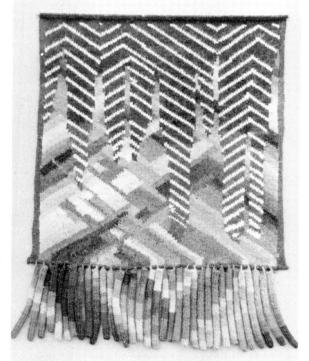

Charting Color Designs on Graph Paper

Not everyone feels comfortable using colors quite as spontaneously as Diane Sheehan. To see how designs can be charted, let's take a super-simple, perennially popular motif, a heart, and see how it would be knitted using a charted design as a guide.

Heart Belt Pouch

Once you've knitted the sample design, you'll learn how to turn it into a handy belt pouch with the help of the next skill to be learned, knitting on.

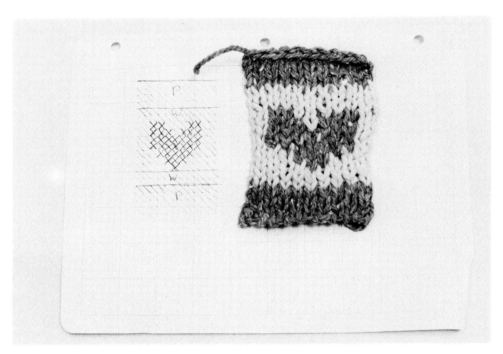

Each square of the graph paper represents a stitch, and each row of squares a row of stitches. The first decision is always to determine how many stitches you want; in other words, to estimate the size of the project. The design motif must then be fitted within this space. Unless you work in extremely fine yarn, the finished knitting will always be larger than the graph drawing.

Here is the rear view of the heart-and-stripes design. Everything is stranded in. No finishing off is necessary.

Knitting On

To turn the knitted heart motif into a bag, you can of course knit a matching piece and sew the front and back together, but why not knit the whole thing in one piece and get into the habit of building your complete form as you go along.

The top of the bag has a regular bind-off, but the cast-on is invisible and this will enable you to turn the flat piece into an envelope. To knit the second side, the heart is turned upside down, the needle slipped through the cast-on loops. The cast-on yarn does not have to be removed, but be sure to insert your needle not only through the stitch loop but *underneath the cast-on yarn,* as shown. In this way it will not be visible when the stitch is made.

The back of the bag is knitted from the bottom up. Knit the first row but *do not turn.* Instead, insert the needle into a loop at the side of the bag as shown. Knit, then turn and purl the first two stitches together. This decrease counteracts the increase made when you picked up the stitch from the side.

Continue knitting onto the side, then purling the first two stitches of the turning row at each side of the bag. Here we see the envelope taking shape.

Besides eliminating sewing, knitting on makes for a strong join. It is not limited to sides, tops, or bottoms, but can be done by knitting right onto a knitted surface, picking up the desired number of stitches. That's how the loops for pulling a belt through the bag were made. To reattach the loop, stitches from the loop and an equal number from the background knitting were put onto an extra needle in alternate order (in this case six stitches, three from the loop and three from the background). The yarn was then cut, threaded onto an embroidery needle and pulled through all stitches. For an extra secure join, the ends were woven back over and under. This alternate loop attachment is like the alternate loop join previously described as part of the invisible cast-on-off demonstrations. Further visual clarification will be seen in chapter 7 as part of the joining of patches.

Knitting On to Fill Spaces

The knitting-on process eliminates another myth about things you can supposedly do only in crochet. For example, suppose you want to fill in a space between two triangles. No sooner said than done. Cast on a stitch, then knit into the side of one triangle. Turn around, knit back, and knit into the side of the other triangle. Keep going. In the illustrated sample the knitting-on process automatically makes your increases for you. If you were filling in a straight piece, you would have to decrease before or after you knit on as you did in forming the envelope shape for the heart bag. Lots more on this concept will be seen in the patchwork chapters and in the shape-on-shape hanging in chapter 11.

The garter stitch section of this sample was knit on at each side of the stockinette shapes. The knitting-on process automatically widened the fill-in shape.

Knitting On for Easier Handling of Large Hangings and Difficult Materials

Knitting on enables one to do large hangings without having to use long and often cumbersome needles, to switch from horizontal to vertical stitches, and to work with heavy yarns on short needles, which is easier on the hand muscles.

This experimental hanging in progress was developed in knit-on style to make the switch from horizontal to vertical stitches easier. The method also facilitated the handling of the "yarn," a plastic tape from Japan used primarily for ikat dyeing (see Sources of Supplies). I liked the tape's pliability and sheen but found it somewhat hard on the hands. Working with only short sections at a time eased the physical strain, but most importantly, made for a more spontaneous progression.

Color Changing and Knitting On Invites Experimentation

B. Joan Langley, whose experimental knitting with raffia was seen in the previous chapter, enlarged the scope of her knitting with the free-form use of color and knitting on pieces as her whim dictated. The subtly hand-dyed colors, and the artist's way of manipulating their interplay with circular knitting needles, are best appreciated by referring to the color section.

The dark gray center section was knitted onto the other color areas. The slight bulges resulted from knitting back and forth several times instead of going around and around the circular needles in an even pattern. The edging is a ribbing of six knit and six purl stitches, much like the edging on a classic sweater.

The previously illustrated piece started out to be very large, but the wool proved somewhat too bulky and heavy, so the artist shifted gears by working on a miniature scale. The "appetizers" took on their configurations through the natural curl of the stockinette stitch, turned inside out, since Joan favors the purl side.

Bases and/or tops were knitted on as the artist's whim dictated. Needles are simply poked into the finished surface for the knitting to continue.

Each "appetizer" developed its own personality.

Eventually all were gathered into a crowd, the base a most appropriate afterthought to complete the concept of joining unconnected pieces of slight variation onto a foundation quite unlike themselves. The colors are the same as the piece shown in the color section.

Sectional Knitting

Having mastered the technique of adding on yarn and stranding in old and new ends as you knit, sectional knitting no longer looms as any kind of problem or hindrance to dividing and redividing a large piece of knitting into sections, to be continued on and joined together when needed. Once the knitter realizes how easy it is to add new yarn in order to continue on with a section of loops left in waiting on a stitch holder, the hesitancy about leaving groups of stitches "in limbo," without the original yarn attached, disappears.

At its simplest, sectional knitting involves dividing stitches on one needle in half, as for the shaping of a neckline. One section can be left on the original needle and knitted with the yarn from the large, undivided piece of fabric. The second section is held in waiting on a stitch holder until the first is complete. To knit this second section to match the first, the needle is slipped through the loops (if you use wooden double-pointed needles, your stitches won't slip and you can sidestep the slipping of loops on and off a stitch holder). The invisible cast-off method can also serve as a stitch-holding method. Just insert your needle through the pulled-through thread *and* the stitch loops, as shown in the demonstration for turning the heart sample into a pouch.

Robin Gudehus's halter beautifully exemplifies the use of sectional knitting to shape a neckline. The halter starts as a straight piece. After the stitches were divided in half, Robin decreased a stitch at the beginning and end of each knit row to shape the inside of the V-neck and the armholes. When each neckline section was reduced to six stitches, she continued on, letting the stockinette crisscross in back, through two loops sewn at either side of the halter. The artist used the stranding in of yarn for the neckline shaping and in a more sophisticated and complicated way for the free-form tapestry design that turned this very simple construction into a wearable landscape.

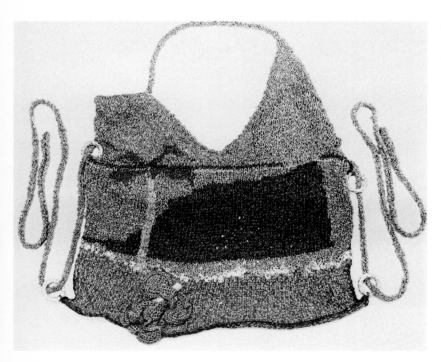

A halter encompassing a whole range of knit lore: the use of color stranding to create tapestry designs, dividing stitches into sections to develop shape, and utilizing natural stitch tendencies (in this case, the curl of stockinette) to provide an interesting closure and body fit. Robin Gudehus, artist.

A Basic Pullover Sweater

Once you really comprehend the procedure for sizing and knitting a classic pullover sweater, you will feel less confused about instructions for patterns in periodicals, more free about making changes and adjustments. All sweaters are sized and shaped to conform to basic body measurements. The following diagram illustrates the measurements needed to determine size and knitting procedures. It can be used to work out different styles and, if elongated, to plan a dress.

Here are the measurements represented by the letters on the diagram:

A-A   This is the width of the pattern base. To obtain the correct measurement, hold a tape measure around your body, reaching across the chest. Divide this measurement in half for the A-A base line.

B-B   This represents the length of the pattern. Measure from the base of the neck to wherever you want the sweater to end.

B-C   equals the measurement from the top of the shoulder to the base of the neck.

E-E   indicates the space for the neckline, approximately one third the pattern width.

C-D   represents the armhole area, the measurement from just below the underarm to the top of the shoulder—usually 7 to 9 inches in an adult-sized garment.

A-B   indicates the measurement from the sweater's edge until the beginning of the armhole.

Diagram for sweater body.

Here is a diagram for a basic sweater sleeve: Line A—A represents the length of the sleeve from the top of the shoulder to the wrist, C—B equals the measurements of the inner arm, from underneath the armhole to the wrist; A—D measures the height of the sleeve top; E—E equals the approximate width at the top of the sleeve (usually two to three inches); C—C equals the width of the arm, just below the armhole shaping.

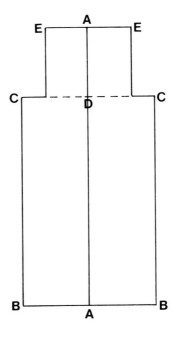

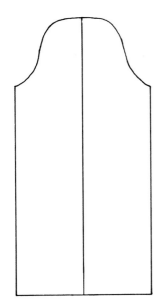

Most sewing patterns show the sleeve rounded like this. The knitted sleeve shapes itself as it is sewn into the armhole.

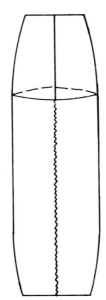

The sleeve is knitted separately and the lower portion (C—B) is sewn into a tube before the sleeve is set in.

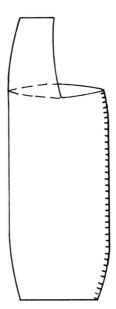

Side view of the sleeve with the lower portion seamed.

Using the Diagram to Make Your Own Size Pattern

Draw a full-scale paper pattern. Use wrapping paper, large sheets of newspapers or plain newsprint, and the measurements for A-A and B-B for the rectangle base. Mark off the other dimensions. Using this full-sized paper pattern as a sizing guide eliminates a lot of stitch and row counting, as you will see when you read the instructions that follow.

Cut out a number of patterns and use as a sketch pad to try out different necklines, to work out designs for tapestry knitting, and to plan patchwork and patch-strip combinations and sizes once you get to chapters 7, 8, and 9.

Knitting the Basic Pullover

Since the sweater is something people most frequently knit according to conventional patterns, the following step-by-step procedures include instructions as they would be provided by magazine editors and yarn company designers. The instructions are even longer than usual since explanatory comments are included.

Materials: knitting worsted—ten 4-ounce skeins, to be used double, #8 straight needle, #8 circular needle, #11 straight needle.

Gauge: Three stitches equal 1 inch; 5 rows equal 1 inch.

When knitting sweaters according to pattern instructions, the stitch gauge is a vital part of the directions. Knitters are usually advised to make a sample swatch and measure this to see if the right width and height gauge is being obtained. If the swatch is smaller, the knitting can be brought in line with the pattern gauge by using larger needles or thicker yarn, or adding extra stitches; if the swatch is bigger, smaller needles, thinner yarn, or fewer stitches can be used to make the needed adjustments. The NEW LOOK technique knitter who has made a life-sized sizing pattern needs to estimate how many stitches to cast on but can measure the growing shape more casually simply by holding the knitting against the pattern outline.

Size: Instructions and diagram illustrations are for size 34, with changes for sizes 36 and 42 given in parentheses. The size is based on the measurement around the chest. Printed instructions usually carry differences in stitches and rows for a full range of sizes, but the three popular sizes given here will give the reader an idea as to how to make adjustments, and if you are not a size 34, altering the graphed pattern will be good practice.

To Knit the Back

Step 1. Cast on 52 stitches (54, 62), using #8 straight needles. Knit ten rows (2 inches) in a rib pattern of knit one stitch, purl one stitch and purling over the knit stitches and knitting over the purl stitches on the row back. Using the narrow needles for this section automatically shapes the waist area. For a fuller waist, use a knit two, purl two pattern. After ten rows, switch to the larger #11 needles and work in stockinette stitch (knit one row, purl one row)

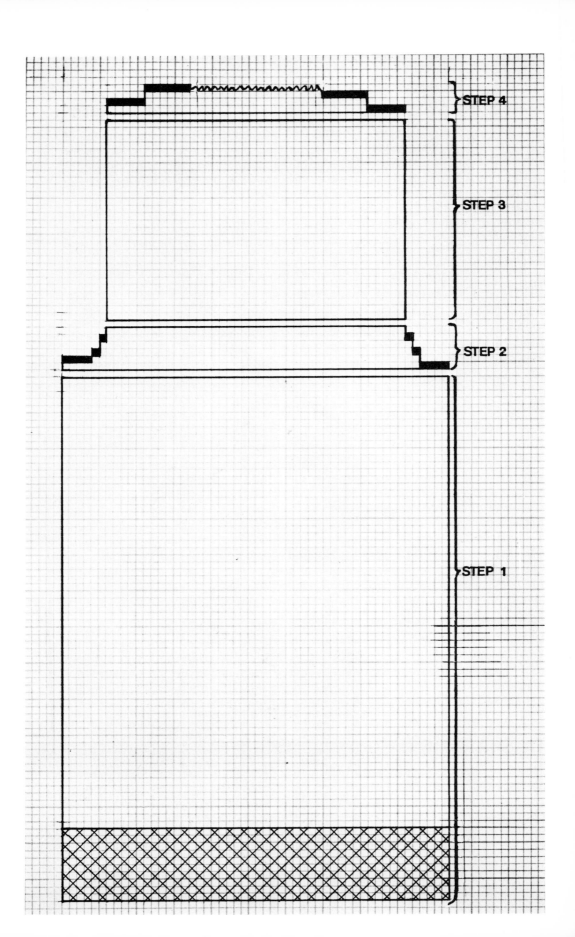

STEP 4

STEP 3

STEP 2

STEP 1

for 62 (64, 65) rows. If using a full-scale sizing pattern, the knitting for this step should equal the B—C section of base diagram.

Step 2. To shape the armholes, bind off four stitches at the beginning of the next knit row, and at the beginning of the purl row that follows. Decrease a stitch at the beginning and end of the next two knit rows. This will leave you with 40 stitches (42, 50).

Step 3. Knit without decreasing for 28 (32, 36) rows . . . or from line C—E or D—A if you are using the size pattern made from the diagram.

Step 4. To shape the shoulder, bind off 5 (5, 7) stitches at the beginning of the next two rows, and 6 (6, 8) at the beginning of the following two. This reduces your stitches on the needle to 18 (20, 20) and these are held on a stitch holder. You can use a short, double-pointed wooden dowel needle or an invisible cast-off.
4-27E

To Knit the Front

Repeat Steps 1 and 2 as for the back. Start Step 3 as for the front but knit only 16 (18, 22) rows. This is just about halfway up between C—D in the basic diagram pattern. You will now divide the stitches in order to shape the neck. Knit 15 (16, 20) stitches and put the next 10 on a stitch holder, and put the next 15 (16, 20) on another needle. Knit each set of the 15 stitches as follows: Reduce a stitch on the knit side, near the neckline, every other row until 11 (13, 15) stitches remain on the needle. Work across the remaining stitches without increasing to match the back. On the last two rows, bind off 5 stitches at the beginning of one, and 6 at the beginning of the last.

Opposite:
Graphed diagram of pullover front. Each box represents a stitch, each line of boxes a row of stitches. The first ten rows have been marked to indicate the pattern of the rib stitch, with the X marks representing knit stitches, the blank boxes purls. Darkened squares indicate bound-off or decreased stitches. The zigzag line at the top represents the stitches being held.

Right:
Only that portion of the back different from the front has been diagrammed.

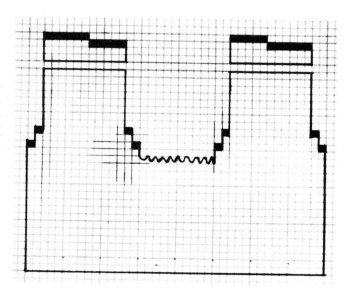

To Knit the Sleeves

Step 1. Start at the wrist, in ribbing to match the bottom, again using the thinner #8 needles. Cast on 32 stitches and knit one, purl one for 10 rows. Switch to #11 needles and stockinette stitch pattern. Increase on stitch at the beginning and end of every knit row 5 (6, 7) times. You will have 42 (44, 46) stitches on the needle.

Step 2. Knit in stockinette, without increasing, for 45 (47, 49) rows.

Step 3. To shape the top of the sleeve, bind off four stitches at the beginning of the next knit and purl rows. Reduce the remaining 34 (36, 38) stitches by decreasing at the beginning and end of every other knit row. When you get down to 17 (19, 21) stitches, bind off three at a time, at the beginning of each row, until nine stitches remain. Bind off.

Graphed diagram of the sleeve. The first two sections are seamed together to form a tube; the sleeve head is sewn around the armhole of the sweater.

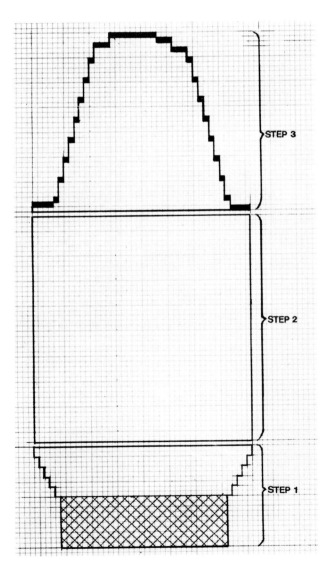

To Add the Neckband

Join the front and back of the sweater at shoulders and sides, using a weaving stitch. Knit the ribbed neckband all in one piece on the circular needles as follows: Pick up the stitches held on the holder at the back piece, pick up 15 stitches from each shoulder seam (use a crochet hook or poke needle right into loops and stitches), and the stitches being held at the top of the front. Knit the rib pattern in rounds, for 1 inch—5 rows. Bind off *very loosely*. It's a good idea to use a larger needle to ensure a flexible edge.

NEW LOOK. Notes and Reminders to Make Basic Pullovers Easier and More Interesting

1. Use a full-size pattern to reduce counting of rows and stitches. Make several extra pattern cutouts and use to sketch in altered necklines, sleeve shapes.

2. For a ready-made sizing pattern, cut apart an out-of-use sweater or use dress patterns (eliminate seam allowance since stretch factor creates its own seam allowance).

3. If you use the invisible cast-on method, you don't have to start your sweater at the bottom, but can begin anywhere. You might want to add the ribbing later after you've tried on the sweater and decided whether you want it shorter or longer. At this point you can work the whole ribbing in one piece, like the neckband, using large circular needles.

4. If you use the invisible cast-on you might want to substitute the ribbing altogether, using a band of small patch squares, or some of the patchstrip ideas discussed in chapters 7 through 9.

Tapestry Knit Pullovers

In the tradition of the intricate tapestries of the medieval guild knitters, Dione King's sweaters nevertheless reflect the modern artist's emphasis on freely developed individualized designs. Since her designs tend to get rather complicated, the artist keeps her "canvasses" within the framework of a basic pullover, like the one just described. She uses standard knitting worsted, doubled. In doubling her yarns, Dione does not automatically use two of one color, but creates interesting shades by stranding various greens, yellows, and blues, much as the painter mixes paints for a more varied palette.

If you'd like to try your hand at a tapestry-designed sweater but don't feel quite confident enough to work free-form as Dione does, make some Xerox copies of the charted graph diagram that accompanied the basic pullover instructions. With color pencils, see how your ideas would work out within the graph outlines. If you prefer, you can trace some favorite cross-stitch designs. Using color pencils will help you not only to envision the finished sweater but will help you control the number of colors used. Try not to use more than two colors in any one row or you'll have too much crisscrossing of yarns as you change from one to the other.

Here is Dione knitting one of her wearable paint-
ings, using a small sketch as a random guideline.
Xeroxes of the graphed illustration for a basic pullover sweater could be used as a sketch pad for anyone wishing to carefully plan a tapestry design.

Dione's work was photographed by Allan Tannenbaum. See color section for another example.

New Directions

Using the principle of dividing stitches and knitting in sections need not be limited to the shaping of garments. Body ornaments, hangings, boxes, and containers, all are possible for the adventurous knitter.

A Necklace of Intertwined Knit Sections

The popularity of fabric and fiber jewelry has given rise to the term soft jewelry. The soft jeweler can choose from nubby and wooly yarns for a sporty, casual look, or lamés and cords of gold and silver. Knit jewelry is a way of creating small, delicate hangings and a good design can often work either as a body ornament or a hanging, depending on the fibers chosen. As we were photographing the necklace that follows, we received a package of fiber studies for large hangings by Christine King. One of these was done in almost identical techniques as the necklace. Seeing the two examples here underscores the indisputable importance of choosing materials suited for particular results.

The materials for the necklace were a rather brilliant gold lamé thread stranded with a dull gold rayon cord. The two materials blended very well and produced a sturdy but still elastic fiber. The design plan was to knit a collar, using two separately shaped pieces, joining both and then redividing into smaller sections.

Each neckband started with four stitches on #3 needles. The knitting proceeded in garter stitch with increases made at the outside edge, every sixth row. Once the initial four stitches were doubled, six rows were knit without increases, followed by two rows with increases made on the inside edge. After the other half of the collar was complete, all twenty stitches were placed on one needle, knitted as one piece, with decreases made at either end to reduce the stitches to sixteen. Next, the sixteen stitches were divided onto four small wooden dowel needles and each knitted separately, switching to stockinette to encourage the shaping of the strips into tubes. Before the tubes were rejoined onto one needle, they were braided over and under.

Gold lamé thread and gold rayon cord are stranded together. The collar is knitted in garter stitch, divided into four sections that are knitted in stockinette stitch and braided before being rejoined onto a single needle.

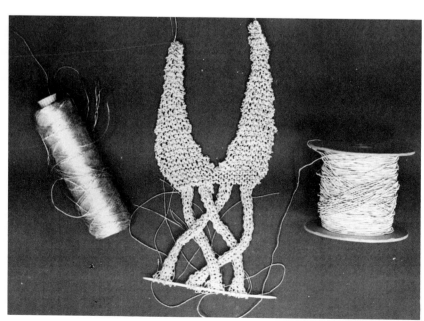

After the braided sections are rejoined, the knitting resumes in garter stitch, with decreases at each side, until there are eight stitches on the needle. The eight stitches were once again divided, this time into two sections that were knitted separately just long enough to create a small open space. To complete the necklace, the eight stitches were rejoined onto one needle and knitted and reduced down to four stitches . . . ending up exactly as one began. Tiny ceramic beads were stitched around the open space with knotless netting, using only the lamé thread. All but the braided sections of the necklace was edged with a row of single crochet stitches, again using only the lamé. This made for a firm edge. Two more pottery beads were used as buttons for the necklace closing.

Here is Christine King's sectional study for a large hanging in heather-toned wool fibers.

Another view showing the pocket created by the artist's manipulation of the lower section.

Abstract Experiments in Sectional Knitting

An excellent way to free yourself from the lock-step type of thinking about what to knit and becoming really comfortable with some of the techniques learned so far, is to work within a supportive frame such as a small metal or plastic hoop. My own hoop was one of a whole bunch ferreted out at a flea market at a nickel each and serving as the start of a series of six. The hoop was easily and quickly covered by knitting a long stockinette stitch strip that formed a natural casing. The beginning and end of the tube were joined with the alternate loop closing previously described (use invisible cast-on-off and alternate loops from each end onto one needle, then weave yarn through all and secure by weaving back over and under). The inside edges of the casing were joined with a crochet slip stitch. The design strips were knitted right onto the edge and attached as desired, again with the alternate loop joining method. You could knit each set of strips separately and sew in place but having the pieces immediately a part of the base tends to help decide on their direction and the amount of stretching and pulling desired.

Unlike the narrow sections of the gold necklace, which were intended to curl into tubes, these bands were kept flat with a garter stitch. The design evolved by knitting two bands, close to one another, joining them toward the center, and then redividing, usually onto three needles, so that the sectioning off also served to narrow down and shape the original bands. Some portions were woven over and under others before reattaching to the hoop edge.

Sectional knitting in knit-covered hoop.

Adding and Subtracting Sections by Casting On and Binding Off

By binding off or casting on sections of stitches a variety of shapes can be constructed in one solid piece.

Knitting a Lidded Container

To familiarize yourself with this method, try a knitted box. Don't limit yourself to square and rectangular shapes, however, but apply what you learn to graduated triangles, i.e., a Christmas tree, dolls, etc.

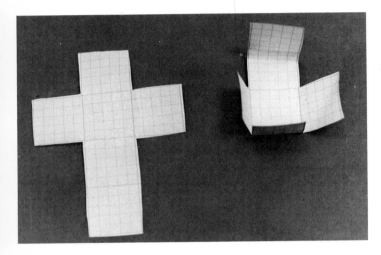

Start with a paper pattern of five equal squares, which will be folded to form the bottom, sides, and lid of the box.

Knit the front square of the container and then cast on an **equal** number of stitches for the right fold-up side. This is done by casting on one stitch,

then knitting that cast-on stitch as shown, and placing it back on the needle with the other loops.

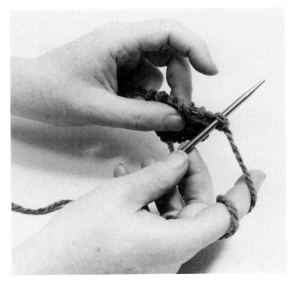

Repeat this until you have all the needed cast-on and knit stitches for the side section. To add the other fold-up side, knit back across all the stitches on the needle and repeat the cast-on process.

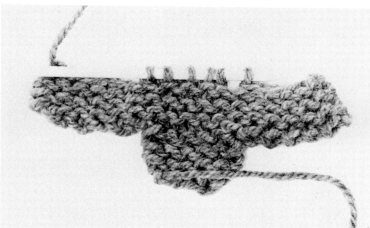

The center and side sections are completed as one piece. The stitches at the right-hand side are bound off. The stitches in the center are put on a hold needle and the stitches on the other side are bound off. Here's where the facility to work in new yarn comes in handy, for as you can see, the yarn ends with the bind-off at the left so that to continue knitting the center section new yarn must be knitted on and stranded in.

The binding-off and casting-on technique can also be used for creating a slit in your box lid (or anything else you knit, e.g., a buttonhole). Bind off the number of stitches needed to give you the desired size hole. Knit to the end of the row, and on the returning row, knit to the beginning of the space and cast on the same number of stitches you bound off.

When the knitted form is complete, the sides are folded up and stitched or crocheted togeth-er. Yvonne Porcella trims her edges with fringes, decorative beads and bells, and

for a fantasy touch, adds eyelike buttons. "Sea Creature" is knitted in bright red yarns, using garter stitches throughout.

Boxes and containers can also be constructed with the knitting-on method. This provides an alternative not only in method but appearance, since you can vary the direction of the stitches, with all the side sections facing in an upward direction. This handsome container by Sue Dauer is a case in point. Note too how Sue, rather than trying to hide her joining seams, makes them an integral part of the design by whipstitching from the outside. (See color section.)

The bottom of the container is clearly defined with stockinette stitches.

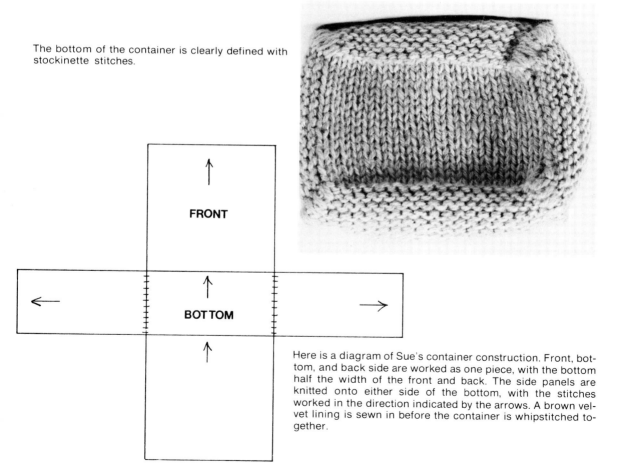

Here is a diagram of Sue's container construction. Front, bottom, and back side are worked as one piece, with the bottom half the width of the front and back. The side panels are knitted onto either side of the bottom, with the stitches worked in the direction indicated by the arrows. A brown velvet lining is sewn in before the container is whipstitched together.

Dolls

Dolls can be knitted in an infinite variety of shapes, with arms and legs made and attached separately or integrated into the base shape. Dominie Nash has tried every possible method of dollmaking. She considers the least successful doll to be the one with a separate head, and her own favorite is the doll made from one piece for the front and back.

The baby doll has head, arms, body, and legs all of a piece. The mother doll has separately made arms. Both utilize color knitting and bits of embroidery to suggest clothing, features, and hair. Dominie Nash, artist.

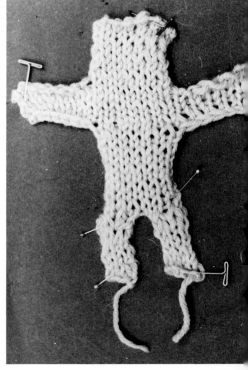

Here is a knit pattern of the basic one-piece doll. Except for the leg pieces, the construction method is the same as for the previously detailed box. This doll form could be knitted all in one piece, just continuing on after you get to the head, repeating what you just did in reverse.

Wearable painting of flowers and trees by Dione King.
Photo, Allan Tannenbaum.

Fabric and machine-loomed quilt by Susanna
Lewis. Photo, courtesy artist.

Garments and accessories, *from left to right, clockwise*: patchwork vest with arrows, patch strip
boots, knit-on tapestry pillow with trapunto, patch strip vest, double-knitted box, knit coiled
necklace with ruffled band.

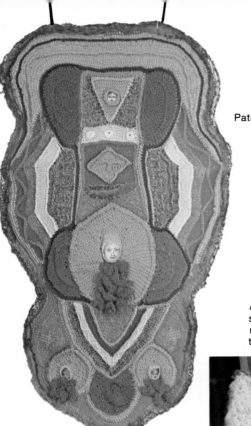

Patchwork of knitted shapes, 2½' by 4'.

Accessories, *from left to right*: free-form lace scarf with knotless netting, seamless patchwork pillow, patchwork box with knit sealed-tube necklace, lacy zigzag strip pillow, zigzag strip drawstring purse, knitted ball.

Afghan of NEW LOOK patchwork shapes by Hanna Wildenberg.

Painted and printed knitting. Dori Graepel.

Sectional knitting in knit-covered hoop; lace curtain mini-hanging with popcorn stitch flowers; "Bagel, Bacon and Eggs, on a Silver Platter." The two knitted containers are by Sue Dauer.

"Oatmeal Mama," a knitted doll container by Yvonne Porcella. Photo, courtesy artist.

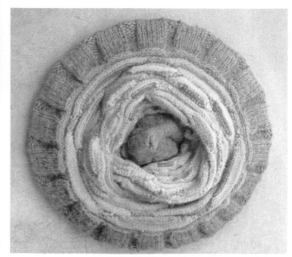

Experimental knitting with hand-dyed yarns. B. Joan Langley.

Fabric and knit sculpture. Nancy and Dewey Lipe.

"The Red Tide." 8′ by 13′ by 13′. Linen knitted on #15 circular needles. Deborah Frederick. Photo, courtesy artist.

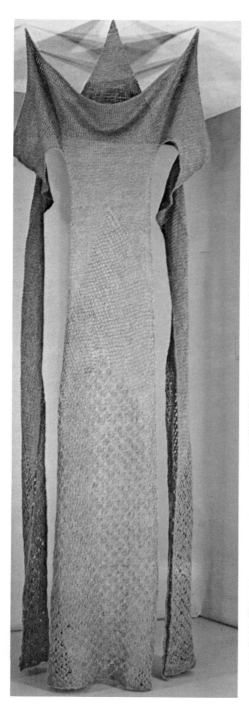

"Diablerie." 2′ by 2′ by 10½′. Christine King.

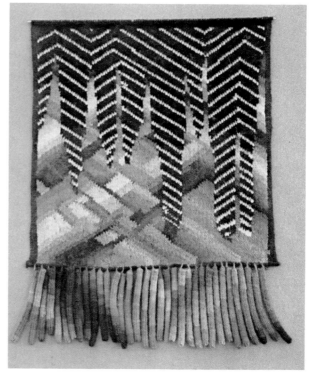

"I Freeze, I Burn," tapestry with spool-knit fringes. Diane Sheehan.

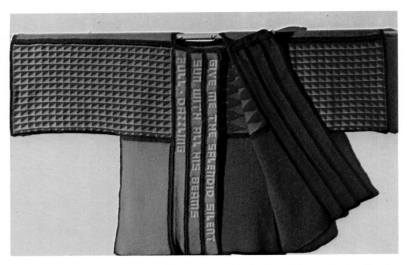

Machine-loomed ode to Walt Whitman by Linda Mendelson. Photo, Charles Decker.

Mixed media coat by Yvonne Porcella: knitting, weaving, and knotless netting.

Patchwork circle sweater, made and modeled by Howard Zabler.

Embroidered and shaped knitting by Sara Lane. 5'
by 7'.

Rug of center-out hexagons and knit-on shapes.
Some crochet and knotless netting. 54" diameter.

Game rug knitted with five patchwork techniques. 6' by 7½'.

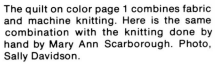

The quilt on color page 1 combines fabric and machine knitting. Here is the same combination with the knitting done by hand by Mary Ann Scarborough. Photo, Sally Davidson.

Loom-knit cape with knit appliquéd hands. Susanna Lewis. Photo, courtesy artist.

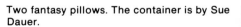

Two fantasy pillows. The container is by Sue Dauer.

"Trillium," free-style lace knitting with hand-dyed monafilament. Hermine Secretan. Photo, Luc Secretan.

5

Extraordinary Skills and Techniques

This chapter, perhaps more than any other, epitomizes the fun aspect of knitting. The techniques have application for those with a bent for the practical, whimsical, or fine arts. The development and discovery of the methods and response from all on whom they were tested have been a major source of satisfaction.

The Sealed Tube

It takes just a bit of straight knitting to become aware of the curly nature of the stockinette stitch. Chapter 2 already demonstrated some of the ways in which this curl can be used to creative advantage. The tube that forms, especially when doing narrow bands, can be allowed to remain loose, looking as if sealed but actually open so that it can be spread out to suit the artist's purpose. There are times, however, when a tightly sealed tube has definite advantages and, heretofore, the way to achieve this was with a knitting spool or four double-pointed needles. Knitting narrow tubes on four needles tends to be awkward. The spool, while easy enough for a child to handle, builds the closed tube rather slowly and many people don't enjoy the process.

Here then is a super-simple two-needle method for making a closed tube:

This two-needle method has the added advantage over the knitting jenny or spool method in that it can be knit on for a very nice edge. Its only limitation is one of width since you can't seal more than six, at the most, eight, stitches in this manner. Thick yarn and needles can give you a substantial tube.

Making the Sealed Tube

Use double-pointed needles only. The shorter the needles, the faster the tube will grow. Any cast-on method is okay. The invisible cast-on is once again recommended since it enables you to add to the tube from either end and pull it to a tight point if desired.

Cast on from four to six stitches. Knit but *do not turn* your work. Instead, pass the yarn across the back and continue to knit. You are actually doing circular knitting on straight needles and thus the front of the work always faces you. The tubes don't work with the purl stitch since you need the gravity pull of the stockinette stitch to help form the seal.

Narrow, sealed tubes make wonderful necklaces and belts, like this sealed-tube rope of metallic copper cord with two drawstring balls added to the end. Invisibly cast on fourteen stitches, knit five rows, pull tight and seam the sides. The stiffness of the cord required no stuffing for the balls.

Using the Sealed Tube to Make Arms and Legs for a Teddy Bear

In the previous chapter you saw some basic forms for dollmaking. Fat yarn tubes make nice arms and legs.

The teddy bear that follows was inspired by a thick tweedy teddylike rope sent to us by Bob Pomerantz of Cascade Fibers. The construction began with leg tubes made with six stitches.

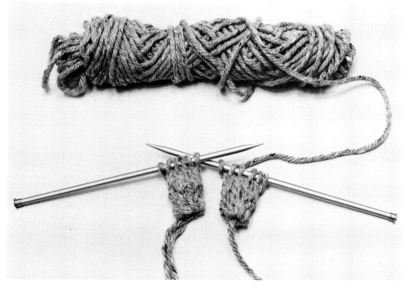

When two tubes were complete, they were transferred to larger, single-pointed needles.

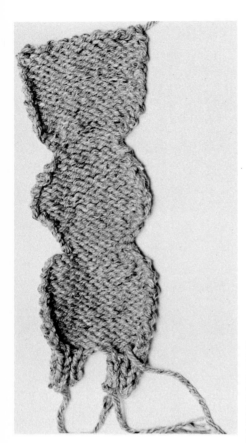

The entire teddy, except for the arms, was then knitted in one piece: legs, front of the body, shaped head, back down for the back of the body.

The arms were made like the legs and sewn into the shoulder during the seaming. The ears were shaped with a bit of stitching in matching yarn. The features were embroidered. Then it was all stuffed with unspun fleece.

Sealed Tubes to Recycle an Ordinary Sweater into an Extraordinary Jacket

Everyone has at least one "really good" sweater gathering dust in a drawer. In our family there was this outgrown Irish fisherman's sweater that proved the perfect foil for trying out a variety of sealed coil "looks." Since it was white it was easy to find extra yarn of a similar texture. No attempt was made to match the exact shade since the combination of different whites makes for a very pleasing white-on-white blend.

The first step involved gathering the courage to actually cut the sweater apart. This was necessary to transform the pullover into a jacket and to reduce the size, for though it had become too small for a college-age son, it was much too wide for his mother. The cut center section was folded in half and shaped into a shawl collar, a base for knitting on a lot of sealed-tube "fur." Long sealed tubes were knitted directly to the cut opening for a neat and decorative edging. This was carried out all around the bottom of the jacket, followed by several rows of crochet. In order to knit on tubes without increasing, knit the stitches on the needle, knit onto the edge of the fabric, and then knit the first two stitches of the next row together. You can also bind off a stitch immediately after knitting on. This method is applicable for any garment or hanging for which you want a nice double-thick border. The man's vest in the color section has a knit on sealed-tube neckline and armholes.

The sealed-tube fur was knitted directly onto the collar. Tubes were varied by switching from three to four or five stitches. To start a tube, stitches were picked up from the base knitting. The tube was then knitted for an inch or two and attached back onto the base by picking up a stitch from the base, knitting a stitch from the tube and binding off, picking up a stitch, knitting and binding off. After this, a stretch of sealed tube would be knitted and again attached. The tubes made this way tend to curl and bend toward just the right point of attachment, which in turn emphasizes the furlike quality. The cuffs were made like the collar.

A separately knit tube of 6 stitches was made to reach from underneath the collar down the front of the jacket, around the bottom and back up the other side. The tube was stitched down in a mock-cable pattern at the front and as a straight band around the bottom. Narrower tubes can be appliquéd into a more pronounced twist or braid, and don't ignore the possibility of color-patterning the braid by using different color tubes, something not possible with a conventional cable stitch.

The buttons are knitted drawstring balls, stuffed with polyester. The button loops are 3 stitch knit-sealed tubes, worked directly onto the inside of the sweater and reattached with an alternate loop closing.

The jacket was lined with a stretchy wool knit fabric giving it enough warmth to be used in the coldest winter weather.

Recycled sweater with knit-sealed tube edging, "fur" and "cable" appliqué trim, plus knit-sealed tube loops and drawstring buttons.

Close-up view of the "fur" collar.

Close-up view of the "cable" appliqué and sealed tube loops and the buttons.

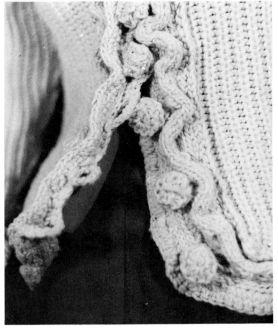

Knit Coiling with Sealed Tubes

If the knit tubes can be attached right onto a knitted surface as has just been demonstrated by the "fur" collar of the recycled jacket, it seems only logical that if the tubes are built into coils, the shapes of the coils can be secured as they grow, rather than stitching a straight tube into a coil. This enables you to really see the coiled form develop rather than trying to hold a long tube in place by hand or with pins. Baskets, hats, three-dimensional hangings, and sculptures can be made in this way. Afghan and granny square aficionados will quickly recognize the potential of using knit coils as units of construction.

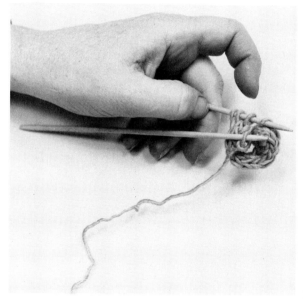

Cast four stitches onto double-pointed needles. Knit as for a straight sealed tube. When you want your tube to bend, pick up a stitch from the edge of the coil and knit together with the first stitch of the tube. Repeat this with the last stitch. You can also make a single attachment in the middle of the tube.

Knit a series of coils in different colors. Stitch them into a body ornament and knit a sealed tube for the neckband. Since this necklace has coils in bright flower colors (see color section), the band was knitted in a mossy green. The ruffled leaflike tube endings are a preview of the next extraordinary technique.

Knit Ruffles

The knitted ruffle was something of an inspirational springboard for this book. The fantastic ruffled things scattered throughout *A New Look at Crochet* seemed almost a symbol of the NEW crochet. Some knit hangings and clothing we saw did have ruffled embellishments but invariably these turned out to be crocheted. A knitting book, it seemed, would have to hold its own either without ruffles or with crocheted ones. But then again, why should it? Maybe there was no knitted ruffle around because no one had ever bothered to try making one. Anyone venturing to take a really new look at knitting certainly ought to give it a try. And so I did.

The knitted ruffle turned out to be easy and delightful to make, versatile beyond belief and enthusiastically received by all who have previewed it. Nancy Lipe has probably become the most enthusiastic ruffle knitter on the West Coast. The ruffles are guaranteed to free your creative spirit and jog your imagination.

Making Ruffles

Ruffles once again call for the use of double-pointed needles. The demonstration ruffle is made with a base of eight stitches. The width of the ruffle can be adjusted by using more or less stitches.

Cast on eight stitches and knit.

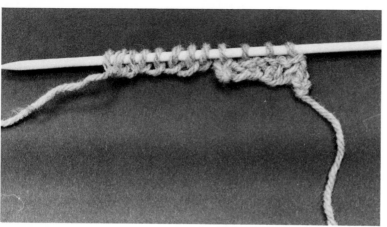

Knit two stitches together, reducing the eight to four. Then cast on eight more stitches.

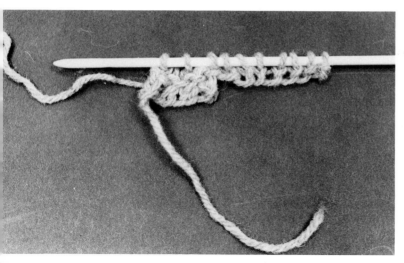

Knit the eight cast-on stitches, then knit two together, reducing the remaining four stitches to two. Ten stitches remain on the needle.

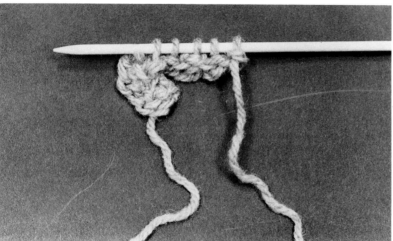

Knit two together all the way across, reducing the ten stitches to five.

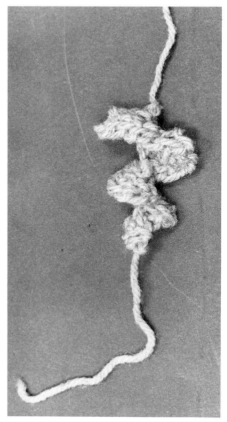

Repeat these steps and watch the spirally ruffle emerge. One of the great technical advantages of the knitted ruffle is that it can be ended at any time. The ruffles can be left to dangle spiral fashion, like the neckband of the previously illustrated knit coiled necklace, or joined into circles. Either way, the springiness remains constant.

Nancy Lipe quickly recognized the go-togetherness of ruffles and drawstring balls. Her lamp base features ruffled spirals, ruffles joined into flowers with tiny knit drawstring balls as flower centers, plus larger balls and beads.

Ruffles are great for the knitter with minimal stick-to-it-iveness since they make fine appliqués for commercial garments. Here Nancy appliquéd three ruffled flowers onto a commercial sweater to show how far a little knitting will go to spark a plain garment.

Pillows, like garments, need not be knitted from scratch. Nancy feels her three circles of ruffles surrounding a drawstring knit ball have brought this pillow a long way from its humble origins at a dime-store sale.

Nancy's small knit sculpture hangs by a wonderful ruffled top. The circular cuplike section is a straight piece of knitting gathered with a seam.

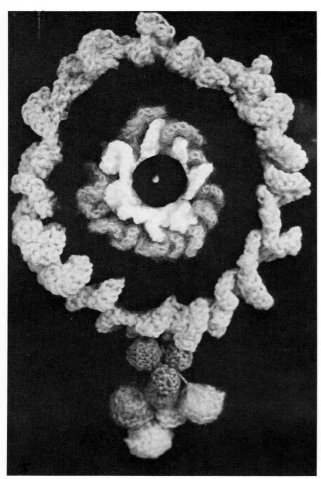

The mandala concept would be effective for a hanging, or

appliquéd to a shawl.

Ruffled Leaves

The exchange of ideas and techniques always leads to the invention of new formulas. Nancy Lipe used the basic ruffle recipe as a takeoff point for a leaf that is a wider based ruffle, very abruptly ended. Here is Nancy's leaf formula, row by row:

1. Cast on 12.
2. Knit 12.
3. Knit 2 together.
4. Cast on 12.
5. Knit the new 12 and 2 together the rest of the way across.
6. Knit 2 together all across.
7. Knit 2 together all across again.
8. Bind off.
9. Stitch veins into the surface of the ruffle.

The leaves emphasize the flowery look of joined ruffles as seen in this knit appliquéd velvet pillow.

Nancy adds some leaves to the balls, ruffles, and beads of her pouch bag. The body of the bag is a rectangular piece knitted in a pattern of knit two, purl two, and seamed together at the sides.

Trapunto Effects for Knit Surfaces

Using needle and yarn to raise up areas of a knit surface combines something of the look and feel of cable-stitch knitting and embroidery. The method is useful for giving rigidity and firmness to the fabric.

Thread a double length of yarn (contrasting yarn is used for demonstration purposes, but for an integrated background and surface design, use matching yarn) into an embroidery needle and work the needle underneath the stitches as shown.

After the base yarn has been laid beneath the stitches, bring your needle underneath this pulled-through yarn and the surface stitches and

back down, always going *underneath*.

To work the design in a vertical direction, raise up the stitches by going back and forth as shown but still keeping the threads *underneath* the surface.

Here is a geometric design on a stockinette stitch square. The dark blue sections in the shaped hanging featured in the color section and chapter 11 are done in this way.

The raised designs can meander in a free-form fashion and be emphasized by using contrast color yarn and wrap-stitching the raised areas by going *over* rather than underneath the surface.

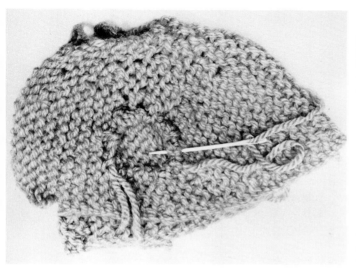

The trapunto look lends itself to the garter stitch as well as the stockinette stitch surface. In the sample, the trapunto area is circular.

Garter Stitch Knit-on Tapestry with Trapunto Effects

The people at Folklorico Yarns make marvelously fat and fluffy yarns in a delectable rainbow of colors. These lend themselves to all sorts of jiffy-knit experiments . . . for example, a tapestry in garter stitch, rather than the more commonly used stockinette, with only one color used at a time. The tapestry is built in shapes from the center out, each addition being knitted on. The central trees were raised up by running yarn underneath the tree trunks and leaf area, filling these in with stuffing during the final pillow construction.

The pillow started with the tree, with the surrounding landscape knitted on a section at a time.

The back of the pillow is a two-tree variation. Front and back of the pillow are joined with crochet. The technique used to make this pillow would work equally well with more finely detailed and realistic designs, knitted in correspondingly thinner yarns. (See color section, p. 1.)

Double Knitting

Double knitting, unlike the ruffle, is well known to traditional knitters. It is used frequently to add an extra layer of warmth at the edge of a beret or collar. Some readers may have seen garments double knitted with each side of the knitting in a different pattern, a truly awesome achievement. My aim is to offer some simpler but equally useful applications for double knitting and in the process dispel the notion that it is something reserved for those with the skills of a master knitter.

There are three things to remember about double knitting:
1. Always work with an even number of stitches.
2. The method is similar to following a pattern of knitting one stitch and purl-

ing the next, the difference being that the purl stitch is not knitted but slipped as if you were going to purl.

3. The basic purpose of double knitting is to create two layers of fabric but this does not mean that an entire piece must be so knitted. The principle of double knitting can be applied wherever a pocket is desired and the pockets can be opened and closed at will.

A Double-Knit Box

Double knitting is great for making rigid containers and a small box is a good way to try out the technique. The demonstration box was made with two sets of three small pockets, twelve stitches per row. Each pocket was opened to insert a piece of plastic cut from discarded food containers. Hot pinks and reds were alternated from pocket to pocket.

Each pocket of the box is made by casting on twelve stitches. The double-knit pattern proceeds by knitting the first stitch, slipping the second as if to purl, knitting the third, slipping the fourth as if to purl, and so forth, to the end of the row. The returning rows are done in the same pattern, always starting with a knit, and ending with a slipped purl. When a pocket is large enough to accommodate the plastic liner it is opened up by slipping the knit stitches onto the back needle and the purl stitches on a second one.

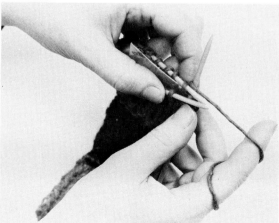

To close the pocket, all twelve stitches are knitted back onto one needle. This must be done by alternating the stitches (like the alternate loop closing). Knit a stitch from the back needle, slip a stitch as if to purl from the front needle, knit one from the back needle and so forth. Continue on until you are ready to open the pocket once again.

Here is the finished box. Three of the pockets have been folded for the sides and front. The bottom and back were stitched in place and the lid left free. A small knit-sealed tube and a stuffed drawstring button were added as closures. The double-knit fabric has a see-through quality that makes the materials inserted into the openings part of the design. Colored Mylar or mirrors would be effective for a box of this type. Anyone wishing to use this technique to make a stuff-as-you-go quilt would need to cover the stuffing with a fabric that would look well peeking through the rather open weave of the knitting. (See color section, p. 1.)

Here's a nice seasonal variation of the box. Make the box without the lid. The Christmas treetop consists of four long triangles. These are made by increasing only every third row. I used a pattern of two garter stitch rows followed by a stockinette row and increasing on the latter, which helps to keep track of when to increase. The four triangles are crocheted together with gold lamé thread, decorated with a lamé drawstring ball.

A knit square is attached about ¾" inside the lid with single crochet stitches. This acts as a closing lip so that the tree box can function as a gift box.

Here's still another miniature tree, this one with red knitted ruffles, gold balls, and a white acrylic base. Nancy Lipe.

6
Fancy Knitting Made Simple

Having gotten this far, it is evident that fancy and fanciful results are possible without ever venturing beyond the basic knit and purl stitch. However, since the more you know about the structural principles inherent in a craft the better armed you will be in your efforts to create rather than to re-create, let's stop for a brief survey of some of the more popular "fancy" patterns and stitches.

Knit just a small square of one stitch pattern per row and you'll realize that the reason so many patterns seem difficult is that the instructions usually involve a number of repeats, forcing the knitter to concentrate on counting stitches and rows, rather than learning to understand exactly how a certain movement causes a particular effect. Once you understand the structural raison d'être of a stitch the ones that seem most complicated will be revealed as nothing more than variations of what you already know. From there it's just a step away from using your new fancy stitch knowledge to achieve your own original goals. Knowing when a variation of a base stitch creates a stronger fabric, being able to zip up a plain surface with an open, lacy, or nubby, bumpy area, are just some of the ways in which all this "fancy" knitting will expand creativity.

Alternating Knit and Purl Stitches to Create Textural Interest

By alternating knit and purl stitches within rows of knitting and/or from row to row, a whole range of textural surfaces and patterns can be obtained.

A row or two of purl stitches in between stitches of stockinette knitting will result in a series of raised ridges. The ribbing that is seen on so many sweater edgings is made by knitting two stitches, and then purling two stitches all across one row and purling the knit stitches and knitting the purl stitches on the returning row. The elasticity of this pattern accounts for its wide use on garments. There are all sorts of variations on this basic sweater rib pattern. You can create a narrower, finer rib by knitting one stitch and purling one stitch; or you can knit two stitches and purl four stitches for an uneven rib. The patterning of the second row can provide still more surface variation. For example, if you knit the return or second row in the exact pattern of the first (knit over the knits, purl over the purls), you will produce a weave very aptly identified by the name moss or rice stitch.

Alternating knit-purl stitch patterns from top to bottom: knit two, purl two on one row, and purl two, knit two on the returning row; knit one, purl one pattern, for a finer rib; knit one, purl one across first row with the second in the exact same pattern (knit over knit, purl over purl), to create rice or moss stitch.

Pattern books such as the *Mon Tricot Knitting Dictionary* (available from Crown Publishers) show in detail scores of these alternate knit and purl designs. It's also fun to browse through old needlework books and magazines.

A baby blanket from an early nineteenth-century needlework magazine illustrates a most adaptable knit-purl pattern. The basket-weave effect is achieved by knitting four and purling six for four rows and then reversing the pattern. Rows of solid garter stitches make for an attractive raised ridge pattern break.

All manner of geometric configurations can result from planned increases and decreases of purls against a knit background or vice versa. These patterns are reversible as you will see if you work your own version of the diamond-within-a-square shown here. To get you started on working out your own motifs, here are row-by-row directions for the sample:

Knit five stitches, purl one, knit five.

Purl four, knit three, purl four.

Knit three, purl five, knit three.

Purl two, knit seven, purl two.

Knit one, purl nine, knit one.

To complete the diamond, reverse above, decreasing at the center so that the background stitch once again predominates.

The reverse side of this sample shows a stockinette diamond against a purl stitch background. It's all done by increasing and decreasing the contrast stitch motif.

Making a Knit Stitch-and-Skill Sampler to Store Tools and Notes

By now you've undoubtedly rounded out your supply of knitting needles and accessories and accumulated enough sample swatches and ideas for things you want to knit to be faced with the problem of how best to keep everything within easy reach and portable enough to take with you if you leave your house. Here then is a neat idea to practice some of your stitch and technique know-how and use up yarn remnants. The only additional supply item needed is a large looseleaf binder.

To make your knitting etui:

Cast on enough stitches to just barely fit the notebook sideways. The narrow fit is to allow for the stretch factor. Circular needles used like straight needles are handy. Practice any stitches, patterns, or technique variations you want. The sample has areas of plain stockinette, interrupted by an occasional ridge of garter stitches. There are several repeats of a basket weave and a large central area within a purl stitch diamond growing out of a stockinette stitch base.

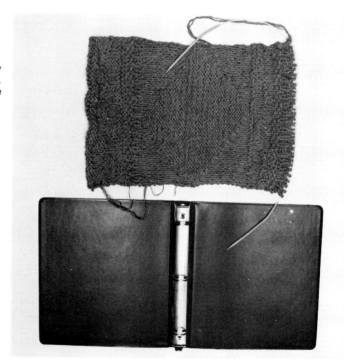

Begin the knit stitch-and-skill sampler by covering the outside of a looseleaf binder. Keep the sample small to allow for the stretch factor.

For the inside of the notebook, two more pieces are knit, this time working from bottom to top of each half of the cover. The outside and inside pieces are then joined by crocheting all around with contrasting yarn.

The needles can be poked right through the knitting cover; stitch holders and gauges and notes can be clipped into the looseleaf holder. A small knitted square crocheted to the cover and lightly stuffed makes a handy pin cushion for yarn needles. It's also a good idea to provide a sealed case for embroidery scissors. The one in the sample was made by knitting on: Three stitches were picked up from the background and knitted back and forth, always knitting on a stitch to the side of the previous one and thus forming a triangle. Another triangle was knitted above this as a closing flap. A hole was made near the tip of this flap by binding off four stitches in the center, and casting them back on the following row. A narrow band of garter stitches, knit onto the bottom of the case, serves as a pull-through to keep the scissors from falling out.

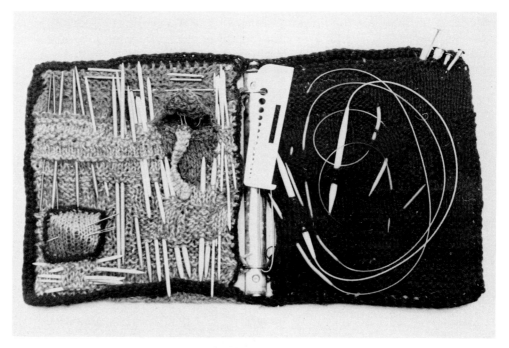

Everything is neat and handy in this very portable etui.

Twisted, Tweedy Stitches for Texture and Strength

When producing large works, "fancy" knit procedures assume importance not only from the viewpoint of making things look more interesting but in terms of effecting a stable fabric with minimal stretch. Minimizing stretch by inserting the needle into the back rather than the front of the stitch (continental or twisted stockinette) has already been explained in chapter 1. Here, too, variety is possible. A tweedy weave results when you purl a stitch, then bring the yarn in back and slip instead of knit the next purl stitch. See what happens when you switch from a "regular" to a continental knit stitch within one piece of knitting.

Christine King samples all kinds of stitches and stitch variations before essaying into a large hanging.

She often refers to the *Mon Tricot Knitting Dictionary* for stitch details, but her resulting work is invariably original. She likes heavy jute for its strength and texture.

A jute sculpture by Christine King, "Superimposition." 6½′ by 4′ by 4′.

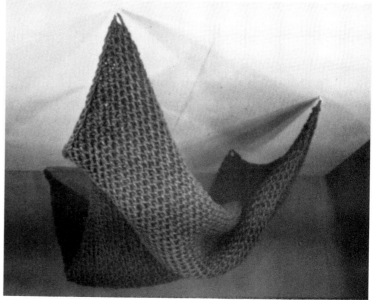

This ceiling sculpture, knitted in jute, measures 1½′ by 1½′ by 6½′. Photo of "Intort" courtesy of the artist.

Open Spaces

The lacemakers of the Elizabethan period considered knitting a timesaving method for helping them satisfy the ever-burgeoning demand for fine lace, but contemporary fiber artists often shy away from lace knitting as too complex. Many seem unable to divorce lace knitting from associations with doilies and counterpanes. The fact is that a lacy look can be achieved merely by breaking the rules about using the right size needle for a particular yarn. A fairly thick needle, say a #9, used for a fine and stretchy yarn such as part acrylic and mohair, will automatically create an open weave.

As for lace patterns, all of these are based on a far from complex principle. By bringing the knitting yarn over the needle at least once more than is required for the making of a stitch, an extra loop will appear on the needle and a hole shows up in the fabric. Hole making, which is what lace knitting

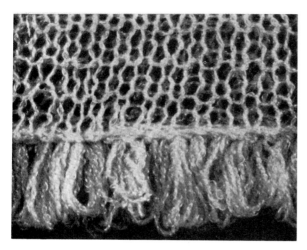

Lacy weaves can be obtained by the judicious misuse of fat needles with thin yarns.

is all about, is the knitter's chance to create with negative as well as positive spaces.

Spaces can be knit with great restraint as to their number or size, or with carefree abandon. Traditional lace projects such as curtains can be given a distinctly contemporary flavor and practicality with the use of atypical lace fibers and colors. The reader's understanding of the lace knitting process will further spark inventive new uses for the patchwork ideas presented in the next three chapters.

Making Different Sized Holes

If you bring your yarn over one extra time in between stitches, you will create a small space. If you bring your yarn over twice or three times, you will be making much larger holes.

Making Holes without Increasing Your Fabric

If you make a yarn over at the beginning and end of a row your knitting will widen at the edges, with the holes making a nice decorative pattern. However, what if you want to make holes several times across a row, and without increasing or widening the fabric? The answer is easy. Compensate for each increase with a decrease, either knitting two stitches together or slipping a stitch, knitting the next and passing the slipped stitch over the knitted one (PSSO). The easiest way to keep track of these compensatory decreases is to decrease immediately after a yarnover. However, this is by no means a hard and fast rule and the way you arrange the increase-decrease pattern adds to the interest of your pattern. For most lace patterns, though you can place your holes at random, decrease before or after, immediately, or a few spaces away, it's easiest to get it all worked into the knit row and always follow the pattern or holemaking with a row of straight purl stitches.

Knitted lace stoles seem immune to the vagaries of fashion. Nancy Lipe's fringed rya version is made with yarnover spaces, followed by three stitches of knitting, a slipped stitch, and a PSSO decrease. All the lacemaking rows are followed by a straight row of purl knitting.

Nancy uses a random pattern of small and large holes made on *every* row and stretched over black velvet embellished with feathers. A very dramatic sort of head sculpture.

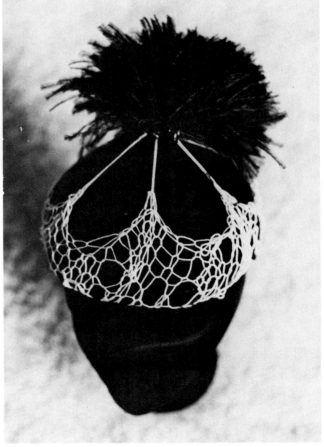

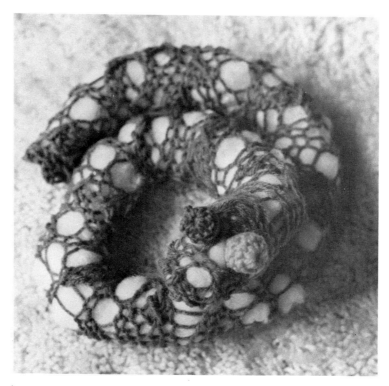

In a more playful mood, here's Nancy's "Silly Snake," with felted fiber-fill body and heavy wool knitted into a lacy snakeskin.

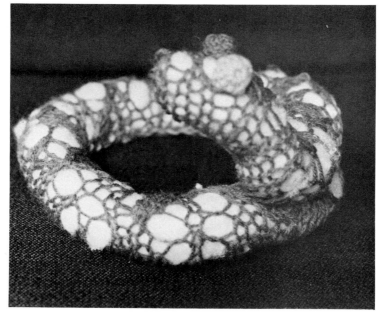

Here the snake rears its head for a better view of the drawstring ball eyes, one coral and one hot pink.

Long, Vertical Spaces

One of the easiest, fastest and most relaxing ways to create openwork fabrics is by making extra yarnovers as part of your stitch. This is very aptly referred to as a wrapped stitch since what you do is to make your stitch, bringing the yarn around once, twice, or even three extra times *before* completing it. The fun comes on the returning row, when you knit your stitch, letting the extra wraparound(s) fall off the needle. As you pull the fabric from the bottom you'll see the stitch grow taller.

Wrap-stitch sample. From bottom to top: single wrap, double wrap, triple wrap.

Above: This mohair shawl is actually a lacemaking sampler. There are rows of straight knitting made lacy by the use of fat needles. There are rows of random yarnovers, some singles and some doubles, with decreases made by knitting together and the PSSO method. For additional lace interest there are rows of graduated wrap stitches, a row of single wraps followed by one each in double and triple wraps. It all began at the triangular point, with three stitches. The first stitch of every row is followed by a yarnover and the last stitch is preceded by one. There are no corresponding decreases for these two yarnovers since they are used to shape the triangle. The edging consists of a border of knotless netting.

Going in Circles with Lace Knitting

Some of the most dramatic departures from traditional concepts have evolved via round knitting. Hermine Secretan's circular lace knit hangings owe some technical debt to that most symbolic of lace knit items, the doily. However, except for the revitalization of ornamental techniques learned as a child, Hermine's series of lace knits differ sharply in their use of fiber, colors, and mountings, and, most importantly, in the way in which the stitches grew into the final design. Whereas the doily knitter would follow a stitch-by-stitch, round-by-round pattern (directions for a design of this size would probably fill several pages), Hermine undertook her designs in a totally free and relaxed style. The materials used were actually the inspiration: multifilament synthetic yarn discovered at an industrial waste outlet store and hand dyed.

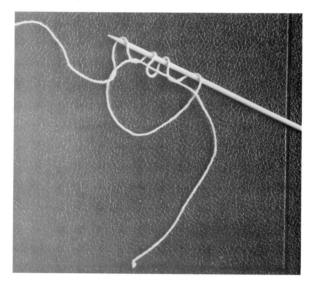

The hanging began at the center with four double-pointed needles. Hermine used the invisible cast-on so that she had the option of deciding later whether she wanted an open or a tight center.

An original cast-on of twelve stitches was divided onto three needles. By making a yarnover before each stitch, increases as well as lacy holes developed. Here is the knitting after its second round, the original number of stitches increased to twenty-four.

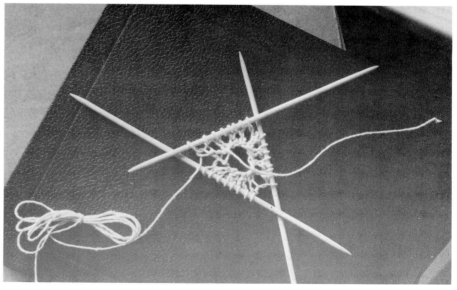

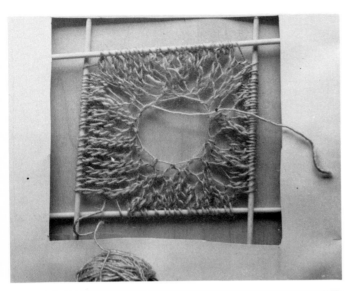

By the time nine rounds are done, dense and lacy areas can be seen emerging. The knitting can continue on circular needles at this point.

From the initial center, imaginative free-form detours take over. In order to avoid excessive fullness, the artist worked some areas by yarning over and knitting two together to continue the lacy look without increasing. The denser areas are knitted without yarnovers but with increases for the shaping. Wrap stitches were used for the fan shapes, with a number of increases made into the elongated stitch. Note the little balls that were made by opening and closing small stockinette stitch tubes.

Here the knitting is tied into the supporting hoop, which was covered with crochet stitches. See chapter 4 for another way of covering a hoop.

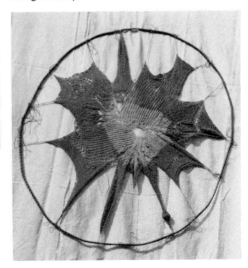

Mounting the knitting into the twelve-foot hoop proved to be very much a part of the creative process, with a good deal of manipulation as well as the addition of some crochet.

Another of Hermine Secretan's free-style knittings, this one called "Yellow Rose Window," stretched into a 3½-foot diameter steel ring. Another hanging can be seen in the color section. All of the artist's work photographed by Luc Secretan.

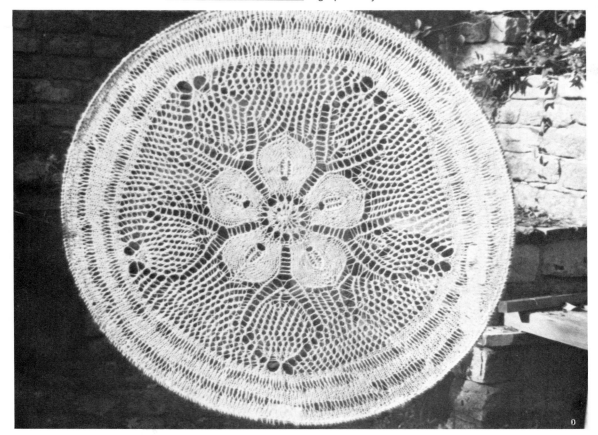

Susanna Lewis uses copper wire to complement her collection of crab shells. Crocheted shell stitches edge the lacy knitting that begins at the center on double-pointed needles. This is an in-progress sculpture, with its final form still undetermined.

The emotional impact of Deborah Frederick's imposing "Red Tide"(see color section) can only be guessed at from a photograph. I was fortunate enough to see it installed at the Heinz Gallery of Carnegie-Mellon University and to walk around it and enjoy the true sense and sweep of the "red tide."

The artist found the actual knitting of the red linen nets relaxing and portable enough to do during summer vacations. She worked throughout with #15 circular needles and used wrap stitches to create the long vertical spaces that dominate the design.

Adding Surface Interest with Bells, Bumps, Loops, and Cables

Bells and bumps and loops and cables, while much admired by non or novice knitters, are usually considered to be strictly within the domain of the virtuoso. My own first knitted cardigan (made many years ago) seemed to me sadly lacking without at least one section of cables, yet I felt too intimidated to go beyond the plain knitting. The first time I saw a hanging with little bell-like forms, the mystery of how those bells grew directly out of the background seemed unfathomable.

Yet many a knitter, using instinct rather than patterns, learns to work the accent stitches by serendipity, often through a mistake. In this way the cause and effect of what was done . . . right or wrong . . . is grasped. When Dori Graepel started the linen wall hanging pictured a bit further on, she was an experienced knitter, familiar with the principle of holemaking and able to plan her yarnover placements so that her negative spaces would form patterns. However, she did not know a thing about making bells. As she recalls, "I wanted to make a super big hole but since I didn't take off on the bottom of the hole what I added on top, the extra stitches on top bulged outward. I was just about to rip out my mistake when a friend came by and commented on how interesting she thought the bulges were."

Isolating the accent stitch, casting on just enough stitches to work the pattern, is another way of learning to really understand the process rather than going through the motions. Working narrow strips of patterns sidesteps a lot of counting of stitches and the general advantages of all patch-strip knitting will be fully detailed in chapter 9. Finally, let's take the mystique out of these stitches and patterns by redefining them as simply as possible.

The Bell

Think of a bell as a detached triangle. The bell is made by casting on stitches equaling the widest part of your bell or triangle, which in turn creates a large hole. The bell is usually knitted in stockinette stitch, against a purl stitch background. If you decrease a stitch at the beginning and end of the stockinette side of the bell, it will automatically disappear or merge back into the background when you get to the point of the triangle. The bell can be any size. Eight stitches make a good sized bell. The stitches that make up the base fabric include the bell stitches.

To get you started on bellmaking, here is the recipe for this single bell swatch:
1. Cast on eight (this is the background).
2. Knit eight.
3. Purl four, cast on eight (this is the base of the bell), purl four.
4. Knit four, purl the eight bell stitches, knit four.
5. Purl four, knit the first two bell stitches together, knit six bell stitches, and knit the last two bell stitches together, purl the remaining four stitches.
6. Knit four, purl six bell stitches, knit four.
7. Purl four, knit two bell stitches together, knit four, knit two together, purl four.
8. Knit four, purl four, knit four.
9. Purl four, knit two bell stitches together, knit two, knit two together, purl four.
10. Knit four, purl two, knit four.
11. Purl four, knit two bell stitches together twice, purl four.
12. Knit four, purl one, knit four.
13. Purl four, slip the last bell stitch and pass the last purl over that ends the bell, purl four.
14. Knit all the way across.

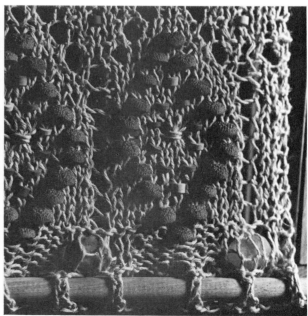

Left: Here is a second bell being started. The four background stitches were purled, and eight stitches for a new bell cast on.

Right: The bells in Dori Graepel's linen lace hanging were an accidental discovery, resulting from the artist's making a large hole and forgetting to decrease afterwards.

Below: Bells need not be decreased gradually as in a triangle but can be knitted for several rows and then decreased all at once.

Below, right: The acorn additions came about as casually as the holes since Dori was doing her knitting while sitting under an oak tree, and there they were, right at her feet, "just asking to be knitted in" as accents for the diamond pattern.

The accidental bells in the acorn hanging gave Dori the impetus to continue her rediscovery of a craft she had taken pretty much for granted since she learned to knit as a five-year-old schoolgirl in Switzerland, with emphasis on perfection in copying a pattern. Here we see the acorns combined with more of nature's bounty and bell stitches used to delineate the features of the "Wood Monster." Note the wrap stitches, particularly the way in which they are used as a casing for the driftwood hanger.

If you look closely at the monster's nose you will see the principle of the bells at work again. The extra stitches are worked right into the base. In other words, the increases and decreases are made the same way, but the nose unlike the bells is not detached.

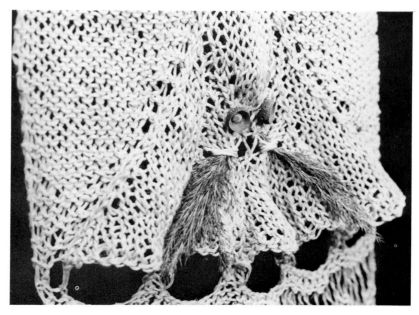

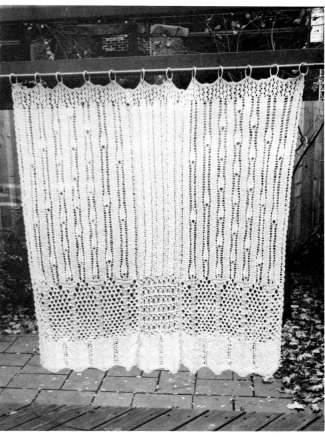

Sometimes just creating something very traditional to function in a way that once might have seemed outrageous or impractical gives a fresh perspective, for example, this sampler of fancy knitting by Susanna Lewis, knitted in a plastic that requires none of the starching and fussing once associated with lace curtains. In fact, Susanna removed the curtain from its natural setting, her bathroom shower, just long enough for us to take this picture.

Bells knitted in plastic hold their shape particularly well. The large mesh surrounding the bells is created by working yarnovers and decreases on each row and placing the decreases in between the yarnovers (yarn over, PSSO, knit two together, yarn over, on both knit and purl rows).

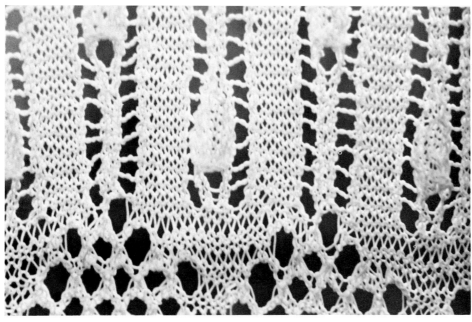

Bumps

Bumps, bobbles, popcorns . . . call them what you will, they lend rich accents to your knitted surface, even if used for only a row.

The way to create a bump is to knit not once, but five times into one stitch, and to then pull the extra loops one over the other. Thus, to give the briefest possible definition to this type of stitch is to call it a five-in-one or multiple increase stitch.

Bump, or popcorn, stitch sample from top to bottom: mini bumps, medium bump, super-sized bump.

To make the mini bump: Knit five times into one stitch by inserting the needle first into the front, then the back, the front, the back, and then into the front again. You will have five loops on the needle. Pull the last four, one at a time, over the first.

To make a medium bump: Knit five times into one stitch as for the mini bump, then turn the work around and purl across the five loops; turn and knit across the loops and pull the four extra loops over the first, one at a time.

To make a super-size bump: Repeat steps for the medium bump, but purl and knit back and forth a second time. It should be clear by now that this method could be applied to really exaggerated protrusions.

The placement of your bump stitches can be planned to create all manner of configurations, as in this reproduction of a baby blanket from a 1901 needlework magazine.

A single row of popcorn stitches made a fine start for this handsome white bag by Sue Dauer.

The construction of Sue's bag is worthy of special note. The front and back are knitted as one piece, starting with the popcorn row. When the body of the bag is tall enough, half the stitches are bound off and the knitting for the *back* portion of the bag continues with decreases on each side. The additional knit pieces that double as decoration and closure were knitted right onto the surface.

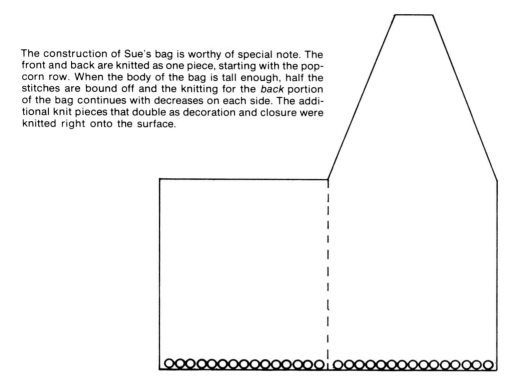

Knit-on or Appliquéd Bumps

Bumpy stitches can be knitted onto a flat surface in this way. Insert the needle through two loops of the background. Knit three times into the first loop (front, back, and front) and three times into the second. Treat these six loops as one stitch. Purl and knit back once or twice, then pull five loops over the first one on the needle, one at a time.

Lace Curtain Hanging with Knit-on Popcorn Flowers

The sample lace curtain hanging is a fun-to-do exercise in fancy stitch and knit-on skills. It could function independently as a small hanging, serve as the beginning of a whole series, a scale model for a larger and more detailed piece, or why not as a unit for a really different sort of afghan?

Here's how to make the illustrated sample:

Cast on twenty stitches (invisible cast-on) of a sky blue knitting worsted, used double, on #9 needles. Knit for eight inches.

Turn the window around. Switch to white wool (use single but keep the same needles). The lace curtain is knitted from the top down. The pattern requires no keeping track. Make one stitch so you have twenty-one stitches, then proceed to knit one stitch, yarn over and knit two together all the way across *each and every row*. Make a single row of small popcorns as an edging for the curtain.

The window frame should be knitted in a somewhat coarser textured wool . . . in gray or maroon or brown. It is done in the knit-on method. Cast on three stitches onto double-pointed needles. Knit three, knit onto the edge of the window, and bind off a stitch before turning. Keep knitting back and forth, always attaching and binding off at the window side. When you get to the curtain, knit right through the curtain and the window. Knit on two extra stitches at the corners.

When you get to the bottom of the hanging, pick up the invisibly cast-on loops from the bottom of the window plus the three stitches from the other part of the frame and knit back and forth for eight or ten rows, until you can fold up the windowsill. Bind off and attach with the alternate loop attachment method, pulling the thread alternately through the loop on the needle and the ones at the edge of the window.

Knit on the flowerpot by picking up six or eight stitches (this depends upon the yarn you use) just above the windowsill and shape as you attach at each side. The flowers are three super-sized popcorns knitted onto the background. The little leaves are also knitted right on by picking up three stitches, increasing to 7, and then binding off and veining the leaf with the end thread.

For hanging the window, knit two loops directly into the back of the hanging, as in the heart belt purse in chapter 4. Use a knit-sealed tube for each loop.

Lace curtain window hanging. (See color section, p. 3.)

Cables

All that shifting around of stitches from needles to stitch holders is enough to make most beginners feel awkward. By using the cable sparingly, as a strip within a solid piece, or a strip to be patched (chapter 9), the complications are immediately diminished.

In essence the cable stitch is closely related to sectional knitting except that the cabled sections remain attached to the background. To once again simplify by definition, a cable pattern is a group of stitches knitted out of order, or simpler still, an attached braid. The cable pattern is worked over an even group of stitches, which are paired off for the cabling or twisting out of order. There are countless published cable patterns available but all are variations of the same principle, as in the following sample made in a strip of twelve stitches with a single cable. If you find that cables are not your thing but you do like the cable look, there's always the knit-sealed coil to be appliquéd to any surface in a mock-cable design . . . in fact, this has the special advantage of allowing you to do multicolor cables since each tube can be in a different color.

The first and last three stitches serve as an edging to offset the cable. The cabling is done on the middle six stitches. It takes six rows to complete this cable pattern, so let's see what happens row by row:

1. Purl three, knit six (the cable area), purl three.
2. Knit three, purl six, knit three. This sets the base of the pattern.
3. Purl three, slip two stitches onto a third needle, and put the extra needle in back as shown in the photograph. (I like to use short handmade wooden dowel needles that are used both for knitting and as stitch holders.) Knit the next two stitches (stitch three and four of the six cable stitches) and twist the holding needle into position. Knit off the held-over stitches. Purl three.
4. Knit three, purl six, knit three. This is the return row that never has any cabling.

5. Purl three, knit the first two stitches of the six cables, and slip the two middle stitches on the holder and put the holder in *front* as shown in the photograph. Knit stitch five and six of the cabling unit, then knit the middle stitches (three and four) off the holder. Purl three.
6. Complete the pattern with a return row of knit three, purl six, knit three.

You can continue the cables by repeating the just illustrated steps or you can stretch out the cables by not twisting stitches for several rows.

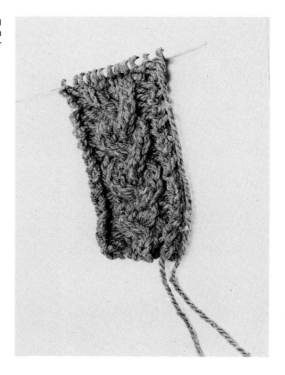

Loop Stitches

There's nothing like the loop stitch for giving vent to the fantasy spirit. It suggests fur, hair, flowers, and is useful and practical as an edging.

Robin Gudehus uses large loop stitches for the "fur" collar of her coat sweater.

She uses smaller more spaced-apart loops for the yoke.

Sue Dauer uses loops as a collar for one of her containers (see color section).

The shagginess of loops and fringes (cut loops) provide interesting contrasts for a hanging of stuffed stockinette and garter stitch knitting by Mary Ann Scarborough. Photo, Sally Davidson.

To make a loop stitch, insert the needle into the knitting and bring the yarn in front.

Wrap the warn two times around the finger and the needle.

Complete the stitch and let the yarn fall to the back. Note that you have three loops on the needle. When you knit back across the row, the three loops are treated as one.

Loops can be knitted into a dense pile as shown or spaced out with rows of nonloop knitting. The yarn used will affect the character of your loops.

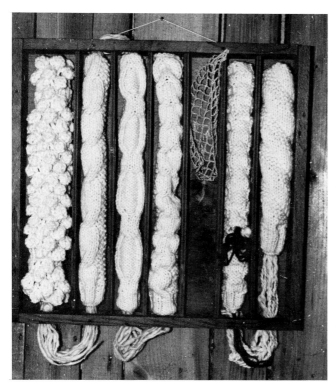

One of the nice things about knitting samples is that they can double as an invaluable visual reference and a decorative work of art at the same time . . . provided you take that extra step of showing them off imaginatively. Irene Reed's handsome boxed sampler of fancy knitting is an excellent consideration for a decorative presentation of samples.

To close this chapter, Christine King's "Superimposition" shows how plain and fancy knitting can be combined to express the soaring potential of knitting in the hands of those able to learn from the past while moving toward an exciting future.

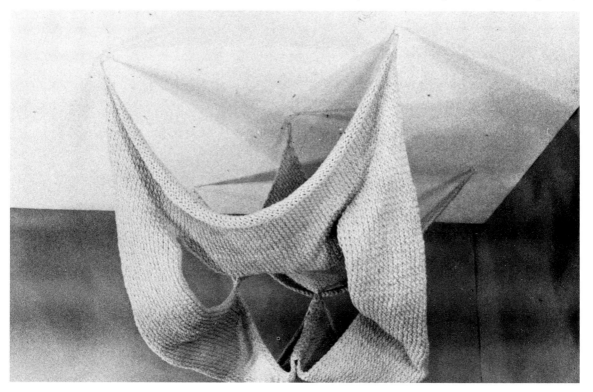

Innovations in Patchwork Knitting: Shapes That Grow from the Center

The great revival of fabric patchwork has given new impetus to the use of the unit construction concept for knitting and crochet. To date, crochet patchwork has been more publicized and popularized via the Granny square. The reason patchwork knitting seems to have lagged somewhat behind is that nothing really new has been presented either in the way the patchwork unit is knitted and joined, or the way it looks.

Throughout this book I have expressed my enthusiasm for the invisible cast-on and cast-off as a regular rather than a sometime method. I feel that by leaving stitches free and open for easy additions, the knitter has greatly increased flexibility in planning a design. The idea of knitting on, whether by picking up loops that have been only temporarily cast on or off, or by randomly inserting one's needle into the edge or surface of the knitting, further abets originality and spontaneity. My development of a different kind of knitted patchwork represents a continual examination of the invisible cast-on-off and knitting-on methods.

The Shape That Grows from the Center

A piece of straight knitting, as tall as it is wide, can of course be used as a patchwork unit. With the invisible cast-off method, a square of horizon-

134

tally facing garter stitches can be knitted onto a square of vertically facing stitches, and this kind of horizontal-vertical contrast can be most attractive. However, if the stitches of squares radiate from the center, the units can be joined in any direction with a unified flow or movement that will greatly enhance many designs.

The center-out shape presented here is so easy and pleasant to make and so flexible in adding on and estimating the size of a finished project that your only problem will be to find the time to make all the marvelous patch ideas this method will generate.

Making a Center-out Square

The center-out square consists of four triangles, attached or knitted to one another. The invisible cast-on enables you to tighten the center after the square is complete. The invisible cast-off makes it possible to add on to the square if you decide to make it larger. It also makes for a variety of joining options. There is no sewing involved in the construction of the square. The sample is made in stockinette stitch, though any stitch can be used alone or in combination with others.

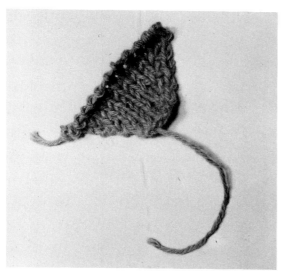 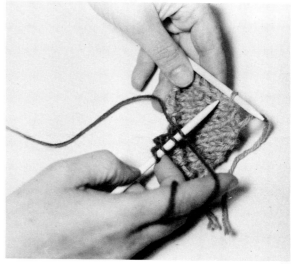

No matter what the final size, the triangle units always start with an invisible cast-on of three stitches. For a stockinette stitch square, purl the first row and increase at the beginning and end of every knit row. To estimate the size of the finished square, double the length of the triangle. In other words, if you want a four-inch square, each triangle unit should measure two inches. The sample, made with single-ply rug yarn measures four inches when complete, with each triangle increased to thirteen stitches.

Start the second triangle as you did the first. Increase at the beginning of the knit row, but do not increase at the end. Instead, pick up a stitch from the side of the first triangle as shown, insert the needle with the four stitches from the new triangle into this loop, which will become the fifth stitch. Experiment with how and where to insert your needle for knitting on—into the center from the front, from the back, or in between stitches. The "join" is part of the look that distinguishes the square.

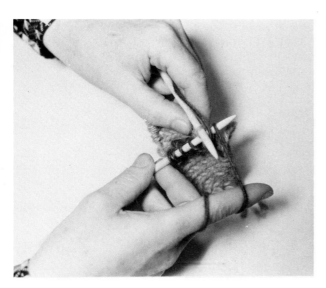

Strand in the cast-on thread from the second triangle into the knit-on stitches so that it becomes woven into the seam.

Continue the second triangle, always increasing at the beginning of the knit row and knitting on at the end, until this unit also has thirteen stitches and can be invisibly cast off as shown.

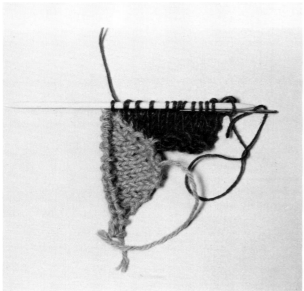

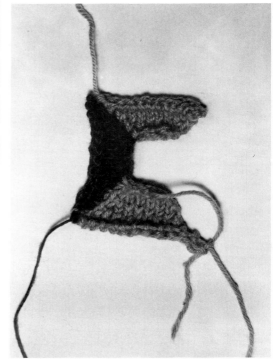

Make a third triangle as you did the second. Don't let that gap that is developing at the center throw you. This is what *should* be happening.

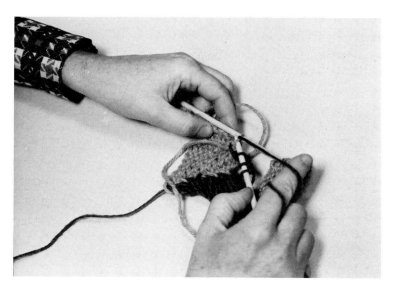

The fourth triangle is worked just a bit differently since the increases are made by attachments at *both* sides. Cast on three. Purl and attach to the third triangle *before* turning.

Turn, knit, and attach to the first triangle. Continue attaching at the end of the purl row and again at the end of the knit row. You will have one more stitch than for the other three triangles when you finish.

This rear view of the square shows how the cast-on yarns of all but the first triangle have been woven into the seams, avoiding any further finishing.

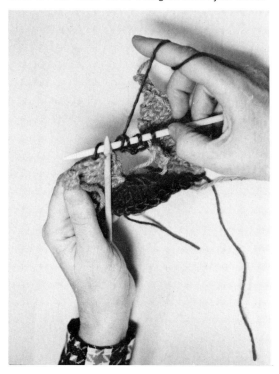

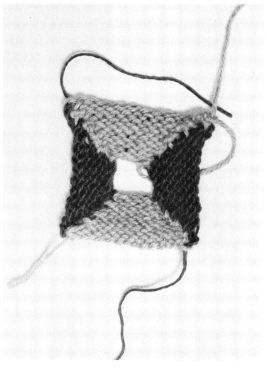

To tighten the center, thread the cast-on yarn from the first triangle through an embroidery needle and insert into the cast-on loops of each triangle all around.

Pull to tighten.

Joining Squares

The invisible cast-off is adaptable to numerous joining methods. For a join that will be undetectable, which is in fact a method for creating a continuous weave and thus a fabric that is a solid rather than a patched unit, a row of stitches duplicating the knitting can be woven or grafted in between the rows being connected.

Grafting Squares Together

Grafting squares is more time consuming than other methods, but once you get the knack of it, the process builds up its own automatic rhythm. The demonstration photos show grafting being done with very visible contrasting thread.

Grafting Garter Stitch Units Together

Grafting is actually easiest if the loops are off the needles with the cast-off yarn pulled out and used as the joining thread. This seems to scare a lot of knitters though, so leave the cast-off yarn in and work with new yarn, or keep the loops on the needle and let them fall off only one at a time as you're working, at least the first few times you are doing this.

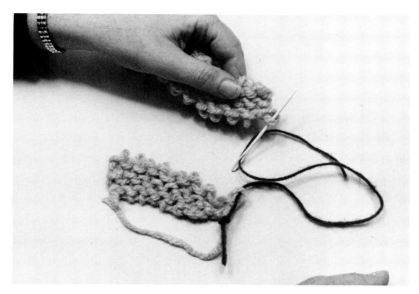

Thread yarn to be used for the weaving into an embroidery needle and bring up through the bottom and the top . . .

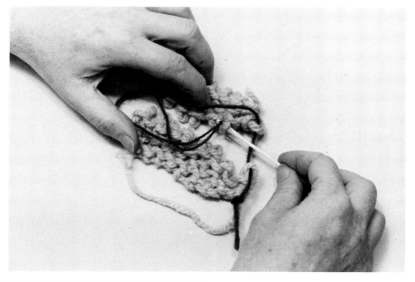

over and down to the stitch to the left,

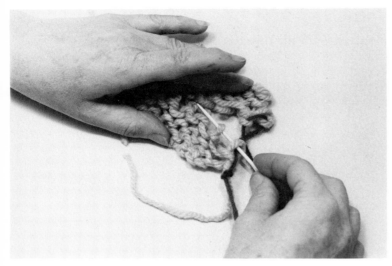

back down into the first stitch, from top to bottom . . . then underneath and up through the neighboring stitch.

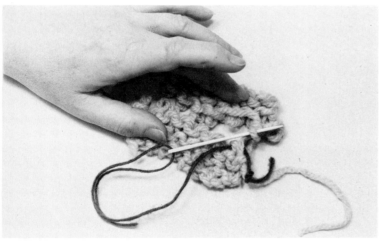

Bring the needle up and once again into the second stitch on top. This completes the needle and yarn's path. After this the process repeats itself, bringing the yarn over and down through the next stitch on the left.

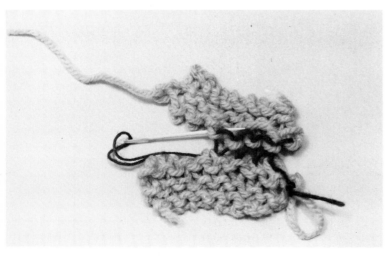

As the grafting continues, a duplicate row of garter stitches forms.

Grafting Stockinette Stitch Units Together

The process is essentially the same, except that there is a shift in the direction of the yarn through the loop as will be seen in the following photographs.

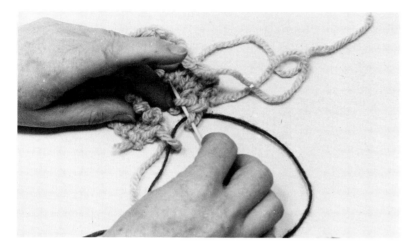

Bring the yarn up at the bottom, down through the top and underneath the next stitch.

The process continues to the row below

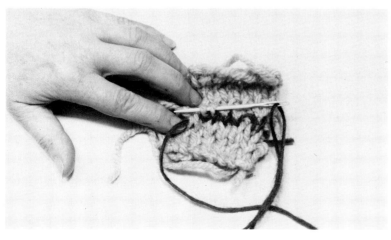

and back through the top as shown, with duplicate stockinette stitches forming.

The Alternate Loop Pull-Through Join

This quickie version of grafting will be familiar from previous chapters. The method will give a flat, ridgeless join. It is not completely invisible but instead creates a slightly spaced pattern that can be effective in certain situations. I find it most suited when joining a separate unit to a background fabric or for very short seams. The process involves alternating stitches from two units onto one needle and pulling the cast-on-off ends through all, first from one side, then the other.

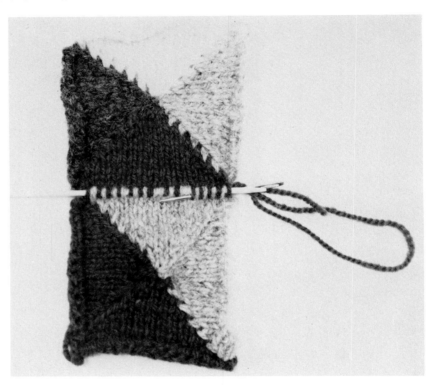

Stitches from two units are alternated on one needle and the cast-on-off threads drawn through all, first from one end, then the other. This method is most effective when the second unit is a background to which a separate unit is attached. The alternate loops are picked up from the background.

Crochet Join

One of the smoothest, easiest, and most attractive joins from crocheting squares together by inserting the crochet hook *in between the stitches* into the bar made by the invisible cast-on-off threads.

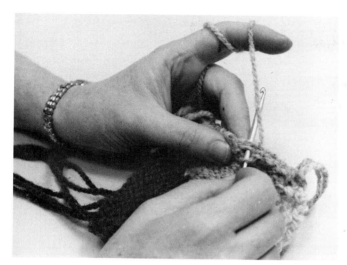

Bring the crochet hook in between the stitch loops and underneath the invisible pull through yarns. Make a slip stitch.

The join is smooth and all but invisible.

A more visible join is fast and useful when a decorative raised ridge is desired. The two squares for this little pincushion were joined by placing the pieces together with the right sides facing outward. Single crochet stitches were worked through the stitch loops *and* the invisible cast-on-off yarns. When going around a square, crochet three times into the corner loops.

Design Possibilities of the Center-out Square

Since the basic square is made up of four individual units, there are numerous ways in which variety can be achieved. In addition to shifting from stockinette to garter stitch or combining pattern stitches, you can mix colors within each square.

The square made up of two half triangles is one of the most versatile design units in patchwork. It is when working out configurations with these type of squares that the advantage of the center-out radiation of stitches will become most apparent.

Here is how striped effects can be obtained with the half-triangle unit. You will find countless other combinations in the many patchwork design books on the market.

An Eight-Pointed-Star Tote Bag

Center-out squares can be patched into different types of star designs. The eight-pointed star is a favorite with many patchworkers. Our tote bag consists of sixteen units. All but the four corner units are worked in two colors per unit—combinations of white and dark green, white and a light tweedy green, and dark green with light green. Acrylic rug yarn was used and the patches were crocheted together with the right sides facing, without regard for a flat join since a puffed or quilted look was part of the design plan. After the front of the bag was patched, it was knitted into an envelope in the same fashion as the heart motif belt looper purse in chapter 4. The handle is all knitted, with twenty-two stitches bound off at the center (this equals the stitches on two square sides) and cast on again on the returning row. Several extra rows were knitted along the handle for strength.

Eight-pointed-star tote bag in green and white rug yarn.

The Lacy Square

This is the center-out square with focus on the open spaces in between the triangles. The procedure differs from the basic center-out square only in the way that the increases are made. To increase the first triangle, yarn over after the first stitch and just before the last of each knit or front-facing row. For the second and third triangles, use this yarnover increase at the right side, and knit on at the left, exactly as you did for the original square. The fourth triangle entails no yarnovers at all since the increases are made by knitting on at each side. The center is pulled together loosely to continue the feeling of openness.

Lacy square variation of the basic center-out square. More openness could be achieved by making holes in the center of each triangle unit.

The Center-out Diamond Square

The center-out square done in a stripe of bright colors takes on a crisp and graphic look. After each triangle is knitted to the desired width, continue *without* any knitting on, decreasing at the beginning and end of each row until you get down to a point of 3 stitches. The finished square will have a regular cast-off edge and is therefore best joined by crocheting with a slip stitch or sewing with a weaving stitch from the back (the right sides of the units facing together). The solid areas can be added on at a later time, and if you do this, be sure to knit through the cast-off thread as well as the stitch loops, as shown in chapter 4.

The center-out diamond square in garter stitch. The sample is knitted in thick and thin yarns in white, brown, and orange.

Turning the Center-out Diamond Square into a Seamless Pillow

You can turn your square into an envelope by picking up stitches from each side of the square, knitting four triangle units, one onto the other, but working from the outside in. This reverse procedure calls for a double decrease in the knitting on of the second, third, and fourth units. Space these decreases out as follows: Do a PSSO decrease two stitches before you get to the end of the row, knit on, turn and knit the first two stitches of the row together.

This square has no invisibly cast-off loops so stitches must be picked up either by poking your needle through the edges or pulling loops onto the needle with a crochet hook. Either method is acceptable.

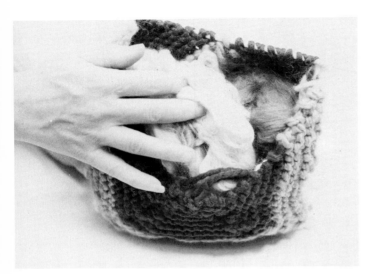

Stitches picked up and knitted from each side are reduced to a three-stitch point. Be sure to decrease before you knit on and afterwards, to shape the triangle and to prevent the knit-on stitch from adding an unwanted increase. Stuffing is inserted before the final triangle is knitted in place. I like to use unspun fleece that felts itself and requires no sewn casing.

Since the pillow requires no sewing together of front and back pieces, the addition of the knit-sealed tube (see chapter 5) is a decorative option. If you prefer to make your front and back pieces separately, you could let this knit welting act as a connector by knitting on to both edges. The illustrated tube is made with a four-stitch tube, knitted onto the pillow, with the first two stitches of the next row knit together. The corners are left loose as seen at the top right corner and stitched into little coils later.

The seamless pillow complete. The slight irregularity of the stripes is due to the use of thick and thin yarns. (See color section.)

An Afghan from Center-out Diamond Squares

I could think of no one more perfect for testing the workability of the center-out patchwork concept than Hanna Wildenberg. She has been an accomplished needlewoman since early childhood. Her afghans are prized possessions by anyone who is fortunate enough to own one. I asked Hanna what kind of afghan she could create using one of the center-out squares as her central motif. The results speak for themselves. The 42-by-82-inch blanket is made throughout with center-out diamond units, using three shades of green plus white knitting worsted, doubled. To diversify the knitting as well as the finished blanket, Hanna switched from large sixteen-inch units to four eight-inch units joined into one large one. Furthermore each of the large squares is done in a different stitch pattern. There are eight of the large units and seven of the four-into-one combined units. Details for working out your own or similar fancy stitch patterns can be found in chapter 6. Another view of the blanket can be seen in the color section.

Hanna Wildenberg's afghan will appeal to anyone who likes variety both in the knitting process and results. Each module of this blanket consists of the same basic center-out diamond square, but the finished blanket lacks the sameness that identifies so many afghans.

The blanket encompasses seven of these smaller eight-inch units joined together to make one sixteen-inch block. Half are knitted in stockinette and half in garter stitch. All squares are sewn together from the back with a weaving stitch.

Hanna tried out a different pattern for each of the large squares. This one is all garter stitch, except for the three-stitch edging of stockinette all around.

Popcorn stitches are most effectively placed along the edges and into the centers of the triangle units.

Here we see a rib pattern of knit one stitch, purl one stitch.

And here is a variation of the knit one, purl one pattern of the moss or rice stitch. (See chapter 6 for details on all these patterns.)

The squares look beautiful with some judiciously placed holes,

or with a crossed cable,

or triangles within the triangles created by patterning garter and stockinette stitches.

Other Shapes That Grow from the Center

With a bit of mathematical planning you can work out any geometric shape with the center-out, knit-on triangle method.

To make a triangle unit, proceed as for the square, but increase each triangle an additional two stitches. For example, if the first triangle ends with 13 stitches, increase the second to 15, and the third to 17.

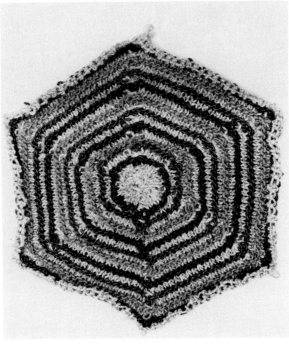

For a hexagon, six triangles must be fitted together. This means that your triangles must be narrower, increasing them only every third knit or front-facing row. It also means that the rows that have no increases must have a decrease either before or after the knit-on stitch. The sample hexagon is made with stockinette stitches, with a purl row every time increases are made, which helps keep track of the necessary increases and decreases.

Here is the sample hexagon built into a one-size-fits-all vest. The ruffle is crocheted on by going three or four times into each stitch. Two triangles are knitted onto the sides. Two knit-sealed tubes have been halfhitched, macramé fashion, adding a closure that eliminates the need for a necklace.

Here is a photo showing the overall construction of the halter. The button at the tip of the knit-on triangle is a drawstring ball that has been stuffed with the loose bits of yarn from this project. The neckband consists of two knit-sealed tubes, half hitched together.

Hexagons for Afghans and Rugs

Hexagons are very popular with fabric patchworkers, and an entire rug or blanket could be made using the same hexagon unit. However, with the knitting-on process you can let other shapes grow out of a group of hexagons and still come back to your overall hexagonal outline. The rug shown in the color section is a good example of this. It is all knitted except for several sections of encircling rows of crochet. The sketch that follows shows its evolution. The rug measures 54 inches from point to point. Its fringed edge is crocheted, but it could be made with a loop fringe described on page 194.

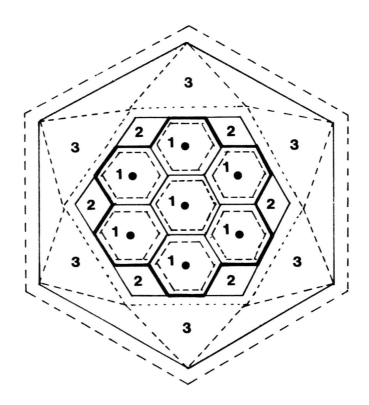

There are three basic knit units: (1) stockinette stitch hexagons (seven), (2) garter stitch diamonds knitted in between the hexagons (six), (3) large stockinette triangles knitted from diamond point to diamond point (six).

The dots in the diagram indicate tiny tubes of knotless netting.

The broken lines around each of the inner hexagons represent three rounds of garter stitch knitting added with circular needles around each hexagon, with two increases made at each corner to keep the points of the hexagons nice and sharp.

The dark lines all around the joined hexagons represent a border made by knitting a narrow band (four stitches) and attaching the band at the end of each knit row, binding off a stitch before turning to keep the band straight . . . and making a few extra rows around the corners.

The diamonds were knitted on by picking up a stitch at each side of the hexagon and decreasing to a point for the second half of the shape.

The broken line surrounding the diamonds indicates three rows, each a different color, of half-double crochet stitches, a motif repeated as a final ending, after the large triangles that complete the rug were knitted on.

The Outside-In-Inside-Out Square

Last but far from least on my list of versatile and fun-to-do shapes is the outside-in-inside-out square. It's a delight to make with a most design-worthy personality. In two colors it lends itself to op-art designs; in three or four colors it makes a nice overall or border design. Try it in just one color, with contrast supplied by a shift from one type of stitch to another.

The Outside-In-Inside-Out Square is equally handsome in two or four colors, in thin or thick yarns. I lean toward knitting it from the outside in, since I love the way the point pops out.

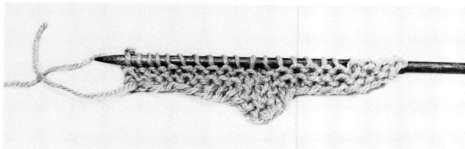

To make the square, starting at the outside, cast on twenty-five stitches (or any uneven number), knit twelve stitches, knit two together and knit to the end of the row. On the return row, knit twelve and knit two together again, and knit to the end. On the third row, knit eleven stitches, knit two together, and then to the end of the row, and return the same way. After the first four rows the point of the square will start to pop out as shown here. You will also have the feel of the pattern and see the space in the center after which two stitches are always knitted together.

To work the square from the inside, cast on three stitches and make two stitches in the middle of each front-facing row, then knit one row plain.

Six squares make an unusual soft box. An orange lining was knitted onto the backside of each square. (See color section, p. 2.)

The Outside-In-Inside-Out Square Stitch-by-Stitch, Row-by-Row

Just to show you how a shape like this adds up in a really detailed pattern, here is the "recipe" for a four-color unit made from the outside in:

Color A
Cast on 25
Row 1 Knit 12, knit two together, knit to the end of row—II stitches.
Row 2 Knit 12, knit two tog., knit to the end of row—10 sts.
Row 3 Knit 11, knit two tog., knit to the end of row—10 sts.
Row 4 Knit 11, knit two tog., knit to the end of the row—9 sts.

Color B
Row 5 Knit 10, two tog., to end—9 sts.
Row 6 Knit 10, two tog., to end—8 sts.
Row 7 Knit 9, two tog., to end—8 sts.
Row 8 Knit 9, two tog., to end—7 sts.

Color C
Row 9 Knit 8, two tog., to end—7 sts.
Row 10 Knit 8, two tog., to end—6 sts.
Row 11 Knit 7, two tog., to end—6 sts.
Row 12 Knit 7, two tog., to end—5 sts.

Color D

Row 13 Knit 6, two tog., end of row—5 sts.
Row 14 Knit 6, two tog., end of row—4 sts.
Row 15 Knit 5, two tog., end of row—4 sts.
Row 16 Knit 5, two tog., end of row—3 sts.

Color E

Row 17 Knit 4, two tog., to end—3 sts.
Row 18 Knit 4, two tog., to end—2 sts.
Row 19 Knit 3, two tog., to end—2 sts.
Row 20 Knit 3, two tog., knit 1
Row 21 Knit 2, two tog., knit 1
Row 22 Knit 2, knit 2 tog.
End off the last three stitches.

8

Patchwork with Circles and Spheres

The circle and sphere are important shapes for freeing knitting from its conceptual confines. Once again they serve as vivid testimony to how a step into the past can lead to a giant step forward. For all who, like me, fretted about the difficulty of knitting flat circular shapes, the dependence on circular and double-pointed needles for making spherical forms, there *were* existing patterns just waiting to be adapted and modernized. The basic circle that launches the technique presentation of this chapter is part of the technical history of the much maligned doily. The shaping is done by means of knitting a number of rows without going all the way across. When the knitting once again passes all across these short rows, a curve forms at the edge. This principle of short-row knitting has many applications beyond the circle; for example, to give extra curves to areas of a garment and hanging; it is in the shaping of garments that the method is familiar to experienced knitters. Our circle will thus serve as a method of learning how to do and understand short-row knitting for noncircular as well as patchwork shapes.

Making a Garter Stitch Circle

The circle consists of twelve segments and it's a good idea to use two colors, switching from one segment to the next, so that you can more clearly see what is happening.

158

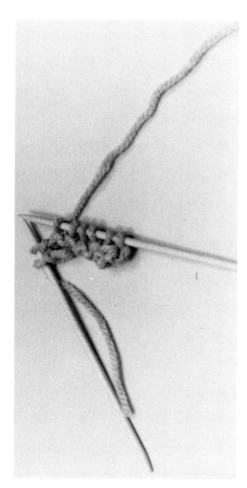

Cast on eight stitches, invisible cast-on. Knit the eight stitches. Knit back but *do not knit the last two stitches.*

Turn and knit six stitches. On the next row, knit all but the last four stitches and knit back on the four stitches of the short row. Next, knit two stitches, leaving six stitches unknit. In the photo you can see that the stitches left behind as part of the short-row patterning form into pairs, so that even if your circle were larger these spaces will alert you as to when to turn back.

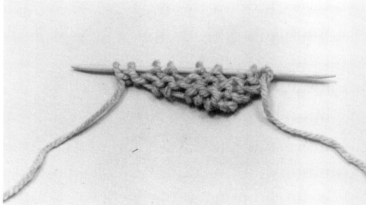

Once the stitches have all been paired or short-rowed, the segment of the circle is completed by knitting all the way down to the inside point of the circle and back up to the outside edge. It is this last step that curves the edge and closes the short-row spaces.

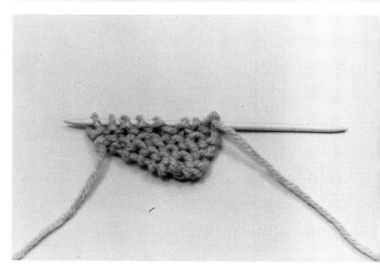

Here are twelve completed segments. The need to join the first and last segment has been cited as somewhat of a drawback by those who wrote up doily instructions for this method, but the grafting method illustrated in chapter 6 provides a completely invisible join, and the alternate stitch pull-through join, though not quite as invisible, will maintain the natural resiliency of the circle as a solid unit.

The center of the circle is tightened by weaving yarn threaded on an embroidery needle through the inner edge loops.

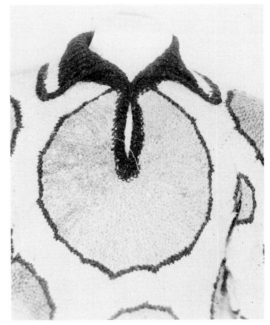

The opening in the circle can actually be utilized as in this ingenious neckline of Howard Zabler's fantastic patchwork sweater.

Turn to the color section to get a full picture of the subtle color hues within each circle. Howard's color changes, rather than moving from segment to segment, are done more improvisationally, much in the manner of impressionistic painting. The garment is entirely seamless, since the artist grafted not only the circle closings but the surrounding areas of circular needle knitting. Note the patchwork-within-a-patchwork effect created with his placement of lace or yarnover increases around the little points of the circles.

Stockinette Stitch Circles

While Howard Zabler favors the garter stitch for his circles, I rather like the look of the stockinette stitch. At any rate, it's nice to know that both can be done with equal ease. The stockinette stitch segments are larger than those done in garter stitch so that a circle will be complete with ten rather than twelve segments. The circle starts by purling back across the cast-on stitches and doing all the short-rows on the stockinette side. Some people consider it a problem that the spaces between stockinette segments are somewhat more visible than with the garter stitch circle. In many instances these tiny holes really add to the designs. However, since this entire book is something of an exercise in surmounting seemingly insurmountable obstacles, here's my method for a completely closed circle.

Start your segment by casting on, knitting back, and doing all the short rows on the purl side. When you get to the last two stitches, do not turn, but instead slip the first of the two stitches to be left onto the knitting needle as shown.

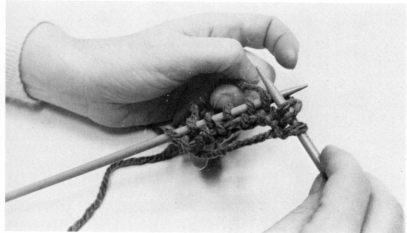

Turn the work to the stockinette side. Bring the yarn around as shown, then put the slipped stitch back on the needle.

Each short-row pair of stitches will have an extra loop—the slipped stitch *plus* the yarnover made before it was put back.

Half Circles

The segments of the circle can be used as shapes in their own right, singly or in units of three or four. The half circle of five stockinette segments or six garter stitch segments is particularly adaptable to all sorts of projects.

This half stockinette stitch circle is one of two that will be joined to make a pillow representing a slice of watermelon. The cast-off thread from one of the end segments is threaded into an embroidery needle and woven through the center loops to tighten that space.

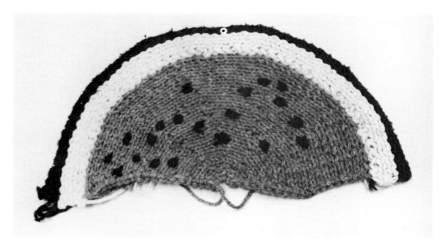

The watermelon seeds are embroidered. The rind and skin are worked together: Five stitches of white and two of brown-specked green yarn are knitted onto the fruit section. (Note: Remember to follow the knitting on with a decrease and also to cross the yarns in back when switching from one color to another.) For the bottom of the melon, a strip of stockinette (two rows of green, four rows of white, a stretch of pink, four rows of white and two of green) is crocheted with slip stitches to each side. (See color section.)

Abstract Curves

If you create a curve at the outside edge of a circle by making short-row turns on the inside, it's just a step further to shifting gears in the opposite directions. Do a few segments as for a circle, but after completing three or four short-row turns at the inside edge, knit all the way to the end of the row. On the returning row, turn before you get to the last two stitches of the *outside* edge. Now continue making short-row turns on this outside edge.

Shifting the direction of your short-row turns results in a wiggly zigzag shape.

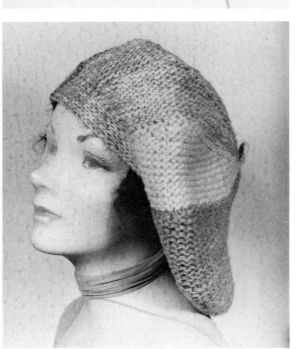

Howard Zabler does a complete set of circle segments before shifting the direction of the short rows and doing still another set of twelve segments. In short, instead of joining a circle of segments, Howard knits on a second circle with the short rows in the opposite directions. When this long, curving strip is joined, the two circles match up, with one curving under. This makes for handsome berets as shown, or a seamless pillow.

Howard worked an extra band of eight stitches at the outer edge of his beret, knitting these in the double-knit method (see chapter 5).

A Mixture of Circular Techniques to Serve Eggs, Bacon, and Bagel on a Silver Platter

This whimsical assemblage of circular techniques is a far cry from the doily pattern that was the original inspiration. The choice of yarns is an important consideration for the success of this type of pop art.

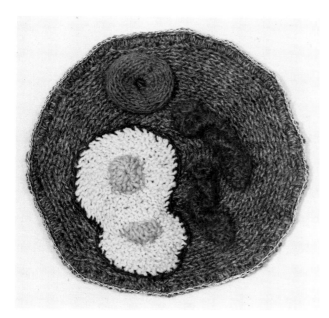

The silver platter is a stockinette circle of steel gray rug yarn with silver lamé crochet edging.

The fried eggs consist of a garter stitch circle and half circle. Six stitches were cast on in white wool, two in yellow. The yellow was used only for the inside two stitches.

The bacon is a very narrow version of the wiggly zigzag shape seen three pictures back. Orange cowhair and mohair are stranded together. Since only four stitches are cast on, short rows are turned more abruptly, a single stitch instead of a pair of stitches at a time. The ruffle from chapter 5 would have made fine bacon also.

The bagel is straight stockinette knitting (ten stitches) allowed to coil and sealed with the alternate stitch join method. (See color section, p. 3.)

Short row segments add nice incidental curves to hangings. This wall mask by Tony Lieberman is made up of mostly short-row curves.

Robin Gudehus used several circle segments to shape the hump of her lovable toy camel.

Lacy Circles

As a unit for a curtain, tablecloth, scarf, or sweater, this lacy version of the garter stitch circle has much to recommend it. The circles can be used "as is" or edged and squared out with crochet or by knitting triangles all around, as will be shown in the next chapter.

The lace effects are executed with yarnovers immediately followed by a decrease. The short row turns determine how many yarnovers you can fit into a row. Here is the procedure for one segment of the illustrated circle:

1. Cast on eight and knit back along the cast-on.
2. Knit one, yarn over, knit two together, knit one, yarn over, knit two together. Turn, leaving the last two stitches.
3. Knit back to the outer edge.
4. Knit one, yarn over, knit two together, knit one. Turn, leaving four stitches.
5. Knit back.
6. Knit two, turn, leaving six stitches (no yarnovers at all).
7. Knit one, yarn over, knit two together.
8. Knit one, yarn over, knit two together, knit one, yarn over, knit two together, knit two.
9. Knit all the way back.

Cupped Circles

If you knit only some of the stitches cast on in the short-row segments, those stitches that are knit as for a straight piece will cup or fall down as the inner circle develops. This makes it possible to knit a hat all in one piece, with only the crown area worked as a circle. Here's how this would work with a cupped shape for which sixteen stitches are cast on, half to be curved or made as a circle, half without any shaping:
1. Cast on sixteen stitches and knit back along the cast on.
2. Knit to the last two stitches, turn and knit all the way back.
3. Knit to the last four stitches, turn and knit back.
4. Knit to the last six stitches, turn and knit back.
5. Knit all the way down, and all the way back.
On the next row you would start a new segment. What happens is that the last eight stitches are carried along or piggybacked as the inner portion is shaped.

The needle is placed to show the separation between the circle and the straight portion of the sample.

Making a Unisex-Uni-sized Hat with a Cupped Circle

A hat knitted all in one piece offers unrivaled comfort. The natural stretch of the knitted fabric will do wonders to adjust the size to the head of the wearer.

Would you believe that this roll-up cap and this perky sport's hat for a man are actually one and the same hat? To prove both are really the same, here's how *it-they* was-were made:

Twenty stitches of double-stranded white Mexican wool (any yarn that will give you three stitches to the inch is fine) were cast on—eight stitches for the circle or crown and twenty for the straight or cupped side. For a bigger brim, this base cast-on can be increased. The knitting proceeded exactly as for the sample just described, except that the piggyback section is bigger. The band for the man's hat is a knit-sealed tube.

The Circle and the Third Dimension

From knitting a circle to a circle with sides that cup into hat or basket forms, it is only natural to proceed to a completely round sphere. Once again, technological help is available from the past.

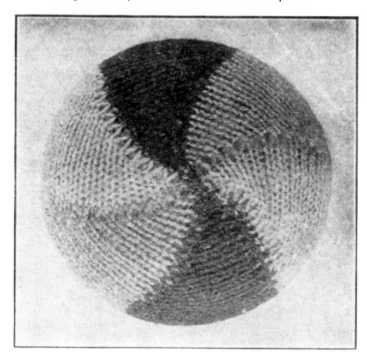

The photograph and instructions for this baby ball were found in a 1901 edition of *The Modern Priscilla* magazine.

Its appeal as a baby toy endures, especially with the knitting done in the bolder texture of the garter stitch and in vibrant colors (see color section). Its potential for the contemporary fiber artist boggles the imagination: A mobile with different sized spheres? Life-sized pillow furniture? Soft sculpture?

Making a Knitted Ball

The technique for making a ball or sphere is almost the same as for making a circle. The chief difference is that you are shaping or curving the edges with short rows *at both ends* of your row of stitches. Here's the procedure for the first segment of a very small sphere:

1. Cast on twelve stitches (invisible cast on) and knit back.
2. Knit to the last two stitches and turn.
3. Knit back *but only to the last two stitches.* You are making a short-row turn on each side.
4. Knit to the last four stitches and turn.
5. Knit back *but only to the last four stitches.*
6. Knit all the way down. Turn and knit all the way to the other end.
7. Repeat steps 1 to 6 for eleven additional segments.

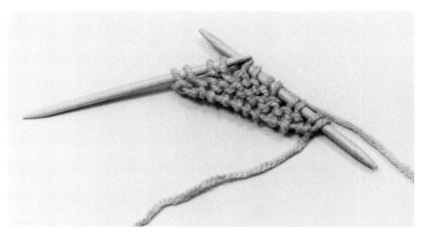

This photo shows the pairing of the short rows at each end.

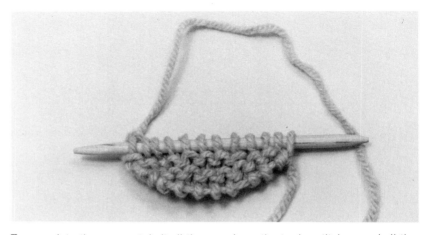

To complete the segment, knit all the way down the twelve stitches, and all the way back. The finished segment curves at each side.

Here we see four segments of the circle completed. It takes twelve to make a perfectly round sphere.

The sphere, like the flat circle, need not be completed to be useful. By making short-row turns at either end of a hanging, an interesting three-dimensional drape develops, its fullness depending on how many short-row segments are done. As an experiment, cast on four times the number of stitches used to make the small sample. Knit back and forth all the way across several rows, then make short-row turns at each end.

When a partially completed sphere is cast off with the invisible cast-off method and the draw-through yarn is pulled tight as the stitches come off the needle, you have a puffy shape that could add considerable dimensional impact when appliquéd to hangings, blankets, fantasy clothing, and so forth.

For those who are not reading this book sequentially, this is a reminder of a less geometrically perfect sphere introduced in chapter 3, the drawstring ball. The large sphere and the smaller spheres in this sculptural hanging by Nancy Lipe are all done in the drawstring ball technique.

The tubes are straight knitting, seamed together. The cuplike shapes are half drawstring balls used with both convex and concave sides showing.

A Star Is Born . . . from a Circular Center

Binding off stitches to continue on with your knitting, as well as ending it off, makes it feasible to do things many knitters consider improbable. For example—a star with points radiating from a knitted circular center and *without* ever having to break off the yarn.

Bind-Off-Cast-On Five-Pointed Stars

Depending on the yarns you use, these stars can be used as units for patchwork construction, as appliqués, or decorative ornaments. Variations in the overall size and look of the stars will occur to you once you understand the procedure involved.

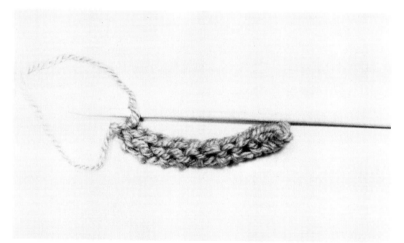

Cast on ten stitches (invisible cast-on). Knit back, then bind off all but the last stitch.

Bend knitting and pick up a stitch from the other side of circle thus made. Knit and bind off.

When working with this method you always need one stitch left on your needle in order to proceed to the next step. Let the invisible cast-on yarn face inside the circle so you can draw the center tight if you wish.

Knit and bind off two times into each stitch, all around the circle. The selvage or bound-off edge of your circle should contain twenty stitches. This allows you four stitches for each of five-star points to be made. For a fuller center, cast on five stitches and do the round of knitting and binding off two times.

To make the star point, cast on six stitches in addition to the one on the needle.

Knit five stitches, slip the sixth, knit the seventh, and pass the sixth over the seventh (PSSO). Now knit back toward the point, again decreasing at the beginning with a PSSO. Continue these decreases at each end until only one stitch is left as in the picture.

Knit the remaining stitch of the star point onto the base of the circle, skipping the space next to the stitch where you started the point. Bind off the stitch made, knit into the next stitch, and bind off again. You are now ready to repeat the process for the second star point.

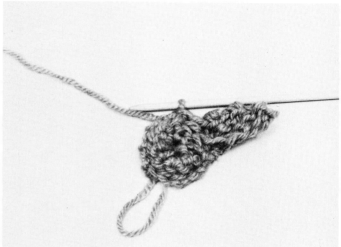

The star at left is made in gold lamé, the one at right in wool yarn. There's no reason you can't make stars with more points, and in chapter 9 you will see one with eight points used for patch-strip knitting. To add interest, the length of the points can be varied ... making some with five stitches, others with seven or nine.

Here is the wool star appliquéd very loosely to a hat made like the uni-sized-unisex hat shown earlier in this chapter. To go with the falling star, a length of knit-sealed tube has been appliquéd free-form to the top.

The knit two, purl two rib brim was added to the base hat with a circular needle.

This pretty daisy is Sara Lane's variation of the just il-lustrated five-pointed star. Form a circular center as for the star, then cast on eighteen stitches (this is not a set number). Knit to the base of the chain. Knit and bind off in the direction of the tip. When you get to the tip, *go around to the other side* and work your way back to the base by picking up loops from the edge, always knit-ting and binding off. When you get back to the base, knit and attach back into the same stitch from which you started. Keep adding petals in this manner. Since these petals are long and skinny and look nicest when they are tightly bunched together, there's no need to count out spaces for the base of the petals as for the star.

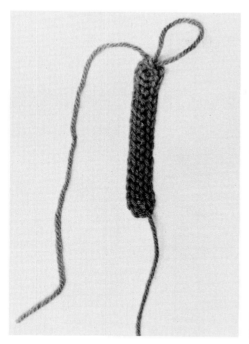

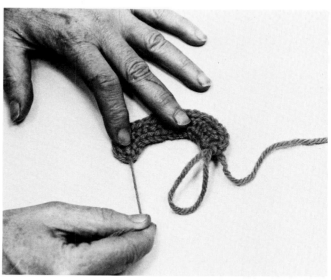

The daisy petals need not be attached to a circle. Cast on a chain of stitches, using the invisible cast-on. Knit once along the chain, then knit and bind off all around.

By pulling the invisible cast on thread, the knitted band curves. This would make still another kind of sculptural shape, but has its very practical uses in the shaping of garments. If you make a skirt, for example, you could cast on a chain of a desired length and by knitting and binding off all around and then shaping the band you have a perfect waistband to stitch or crochet in place. This would work equally well for sleeves, collars, etc.

Here is yet another variation on the cast-on-bind-off theme, again by Sara Lane. A length of stitches is cast on. Depending on the project at hand, this chain can be formed into a circle or left flat. Once again, stitches are cast on. This time, instead of knitting back toward the base and then knitting and binding off all around, the knitting and binding off is immediate, just once from the tip to the base. Petals are picked up and knitted from either side of the chain and in random lengths, and a very distinctive sort of ruffle results. This should be of special interest to all who enjoyed the ruffle introduced in chapter 5. Sara's experiment was done in plush velour, embroidered with tiny seashells. It all makes for a most attractive body ornament.

When the velour neckpiece is pulled closely around the neck, it becomes a cozy and eye-catching neck scarf. The hat is a brimmed and bobbled stockinette stitch variation of the garter stitch hats seen earlier in this chapter.

Details for the Brimmed, Bobble-Stitched Hat

The crown of the hat was made exactly like the uni-sized, unisex hat earlier in this chapter—twenty stitches, with eight worked like a circle, and twelve carried without shaping. There are ten rather than twelve segments because the stockinette stitch is used. The bobble stitches (see chapter 6) were planned as follows: After the first short-row turn, a bobble stitch was made into the middle of the twelve carry-along stitches (stitch seven). On the next stockinette row, two bobbles were made, one into stitch six and one into stitch eight. On the following row, a single bobble was once again made into stitch seven. The end of the bobble grouping coincides with the end of the circle segment.

The brim was knitted separately, a band of straight knitting. I used eight stitches for a medium brim. A wider brim could be made using twelve or more stitches. When knitting in the round with circular needles a brim like this would be increased at spaced intervals to give the proper fullness as the brim expands. Here, with the entire width of the band knitted at once, using straight needles, the fullness is achieved by means of interspersing a segment of short rows, as for the circle of the crown ... ten such segments, one for each segment in the crown will give just the right fullness. If you keep holding the brim up against the hat you can use the bobbles as a guide. Just switch from straight knitting to one short-row segment every time you get to the beginning of a group of bobbles. A wider brim with more stitches would entail a wider segment so the procedure is the same no matter how many stitches you use for the brim. The beginning and end of the brim must be joined, as you joined the crown of the hat. The brim is attached to the crown with a row of single crochet stitches, worked along the outside to raise a decorative and solid hatband ridge.

9 Patch-Strip Knitting

Vertical or horizontal bands or strips provide all the advantages of other types of patchwork knitting, notably, ease and comfort and portability. Moreover, the patch-strip look is a very distinctive one, with its own smooth and flowing grace. The figure flattering properties of patch-strip knitting will be especially appreciated by anyone who yearns to look taller and thinner. . . and who doesn't? The patch strip's value for garment construction alone would make it worth spotlighting. Its uses beyond clothing are myriad: art hangings, afghans, curtains and dividers, table covers, scarves, etc. The illustrations and suggestions offered here are merely the tip of the iceberg, launching points for your own ideas. The patch strips can be used in combination with other forms and techniques—sewn, crocheted together or knit, one right onto another.

Crochet Patched Garter Stitch Bands

I've always loved the bouncy texture of the garter stitch, its honesty and strength and the way it shows off the tone and color of yarn. Apparently more and more knitters share this feeling. According to a friend who operates a yarn shop, the garter stitch has been rivaling the stockinette stitch in popularity, after years of the latter's greater popularity as a "finer, classier"-

looking stitch. For patch-strip knitting, the garter stitch provides a wonderfully even edge, perfect for joining with crochet, especially if the crocheting is done on the right side (the wrong sides of the bands facing in as you crochet) and thus forming an accent ridge that pulls the bands together visually as well as structurally.

I can think of no better illustration of the pleasantness and ease of designing with crocheted patched garter stitch bands than Pamela Richardson's simple yet simply marvelous three-quarter coat. It is constructed of 18 bands, only two of which require a very minimal amount of shaping for the neckline. There is absolutely no sewing since crochet is the constructional and color unifier. Pam knitted most of the strips on the subway, while going to and from her job at the Village Yarn Center in New York's Greenwich Village. It was there too that Pam selected the soft hues of light red, blue, and gold of Bergä-Ullman's Gute Melange yarn. She knitted the single-ply yarn with large needles to obtain an airy weave. The photos of Pam modeling her jacket are by Greg Gendall.

This straight sleeve derives from a classic Mideastern garment design popular with many knitters. The fullness makes it easy to layer the coat over other sweaters during extremely cold weather. Lining knitted jackets is a good idea for severe climates, but be sure to use a stretchy knit material. Another possibility for double warmth is to make two sets of bands and crochet them together all at once. This would give you a double-layered, reversible coat.

Pam finds the mid-knee length very flexible. She found making the longest band to measure sixty inches just right for her medium height. For the not-so-thin this type of coat can be given a gentle and flattering flare. To do so, widen the strips, two stitches a row at six-inch intervals between hem and armhole.

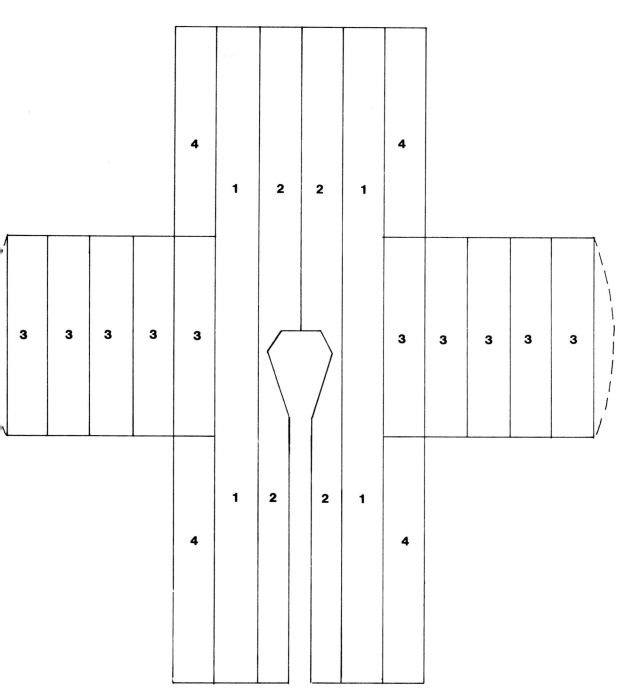

This sketch shows the patch-strip construction. As you can see, both the front and back of the garment can be done as a single unit with this method. The shaping of the number two strips is a matter of decreasing at one side, and then increasing the same amount. A decrease of two stitches at a time, to half the width of the strip, should be about right. The side bands (number four) are crocheted onto the first of the five bands that comprise each sleeve. The width of the armband is a matter of personal preference. Pam found her own eighteen-inch bands just a bit too big.

Fancy Stitches Make Great Patch Strips

As discussed in chapter 6 novice knitters are generally put off by patterns that demand their keeping track of a lot of stitches and this not only intimidates but prevents understanding of the basic and usually very uncomplicated principles at play in the creation of the so-called fancy stitches. At this point you probably concluded for yourself that many of those sample strips of a single repeat of something like the crossed cable strip could be easily adapted to patch-strip knitting.

Nancy Lipe accentuates a commercially knit cap with a band of cable stitches, plus three graduated ruffles joined to form circles (see chapters 5 and 6 for details on cables and ruffles).

The Strip Approach to Square or Round Modules

Since sewing patched squares into strips and joining these together is a standard fabric patchwork procedure, let's consider smaller shapes as components for patch strips.

Here is the star introduced in the last chapter, this time with eight instead of five points. The points are made with special consideration for patch stripping: Four of the points are made with a seven-stitch base, four are made with just five stitches. The center could have been made like the originally illustrated star, but to try out a different look I started this one with a garter stitch circle, using just six stitches for the segments. This type of center provides an outside edge of twenty-four loops so that there are three loops into which to fit each star point.

The sketch illustrates how the shorter star points are used to align the stars into a row that is easily stitched together. A knit-sealed tube can be attached at the short points at the top and bottom. These open strips are ideal for nostalgia enthusiasts and combine well to make lacy tablecloths, curtains, or afghans. Done in bright modern colors and hung individually, they could make a modern divider.

Triangles and Rectangles in a Row

Let's take yet another look at the star, not as a motif to be constructed into a patch strip but to see how the vertically knitted triangles that make up the star points can also be knitted off flat bands. The great advantage of this method is that a continuous series of geometric motifs can be knitted directly off a flat band (or any straight base) without breaking off the yarn. The vertical pattern of the stitches is a nice change from the more typical triangle look. The knit-on-bind-off attachment method adds an additional bit of texture that may require some visual adjustment on the part of knitters locked into the requirements for the "perfect" smooth surface. Care in knitting and blocking of the finished work can erase joining ridges though I personally don't even try for a perfect join since I like to raise up the areas around the additions with an extra row of crochet or knotless netting. The triangles and rectangles knit in a row actually help define where best to add surface interest.

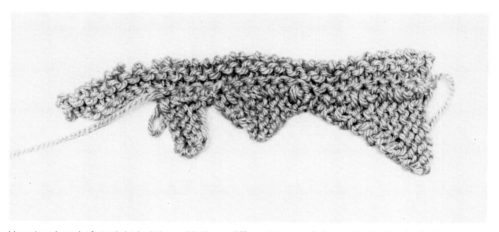

Here is a band of straight knitting with three different types of shapes knitted onto the bound-off edge, all in a row, without breaking the thread. From right to left:
1. The diagonally decreased triangle is made by picking up a stitch from the base and casting on enough additional stitches to equal the desired length of the triangle. For example, cast on seven stitches, knit back and onto the base and bind off the extra stitch thus made. Knit five stitches, PSSO. Turn and knit six, attach, and bind off another stitch. Continue knitting on and binding off a stitch at the base, and reducing one at the tip until only two stitches are left. Bind these off and cast on again for the next triangle.
2. The middle triangle starts with the one stitch from the base plus one cast-on. Knit two, attach, and bind off. Now knit back toward the point and make or increase a stitch. Keep attaching and binding off at the base and increasing at the point until the triangle has the desired height. Then, decrease a stitch before getting to the point until you get back down to two stitches. Bind off, knit, and bind off into the base.
3. The rectangular form is made by casting on the desired number of stitches and knitting back and forth, attaching and binding off a stitch at the base. When the shape is the desired width, bind off all the way down to the base. You can make larger spaces in between the shapes in a row by knitting and binding off into the base several times.

Patch Strips and Squares Team Up for a Vest Requiring No Pattern

By starting a garment at the center and building sideways, upward, and downward, the shape grows very naturally without need for a pattern. Another vest, a paper pattern, a garment cut apart. . . any of these serve as guidelines for the way things will fit.

This man's vest began with a center-out diamond square. An old vest is used as a sizing guide. A band of stockinette stitches were knit to the top and bottom of the shape, and then along each side. Garter strip bands are knitted on at each side. The invisible cast-on bottom will allow the vest to continue its growth pattern.

The bottom of the vest shows the triangles-in-a-row in action. The triangles make a perfect base for knitted-on arrows. The arrow tops were knitted first, with stitches picked up from each side of the strip triangles. When the arrow tops were filled in, the arrow stems were added (the invisible cast-off and stranding yarn ends as part of the knitting makes this a quick and easy procedure). The lighter garter stitch areas were filled in by knitting from side to side. The knit one, purl one rib edging was worked all around the sweater on circular needles (front and back are identical except for a reversal of colors in the central square). (See color section.)

Several details complete this wearable technique sampler: knotless netting adds surface interest all around the central square and the arrows. The neckline and armholes are finished with a knitted-on knit-sealed tube.

Diagonal Strips

If you made the sample on page 108, chapter 6, used to illustrate contrast stitch increases and decreases to create geometric patterns within a one-color knitted surface, you've already done some of what knitting histories refer to as diagonal or bias knitting. The patterns are always a focus on the emerging central shapes and the diagonal is formed by increasing at one side and decreasing at the other.

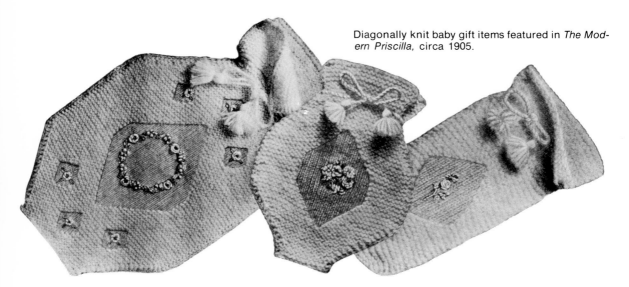

Diagonally knit baby gift items featured in *The Modern Priscilla*, circa 1905.

Diagonal strip knitting focuses on the stitches that frame the central areas of traditional bias knitting. The frame is divided in half and each half is knitted separately so that very short needles can be used. The diagonal is made by increasing at one side, decreasing at the other, and then reversing the increase-decrease procedure.

Two diagonal strips can be joined by pulling the invisible cast-on-off yarns through the loops and securing with an additional back and forth weave-in of the yarn. Here four-ply jute is knitted on extra-thick dowel needles to form two strips that measure two feet in height even though only twelve stitches are on the needle as each strip is being knitted.

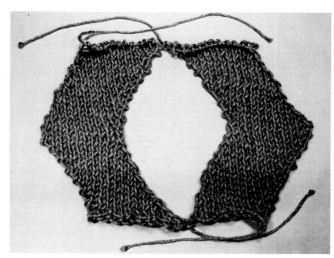

The finished hanging measures three feet by six feet. The strips were placed on wooden dowels, stained a soft green to blend with the variegated greenish brown mohair insert knitted with a random pattern of small and large holes. The edges of the hanging are finger looped and the long lengths of unraveled jute larksheaded to the bottom dowel.

Continuous Diagonal Strips

The diagonal strips can be extended zigzag fashion by repeating the pattern. These extended zigzag diagonal strips are particularly adaptable for garments and hangings.

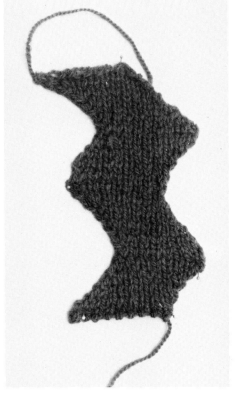

Continuous diagonal strip.

Diagonal Strip Arrow Vest

The arrow vest started with the idea of using vertically and horizontally placed diagonal strips to both diversify and unify the front and back of the garment. The arrows evolved from the open areas. A paper pattern was used as a guide.

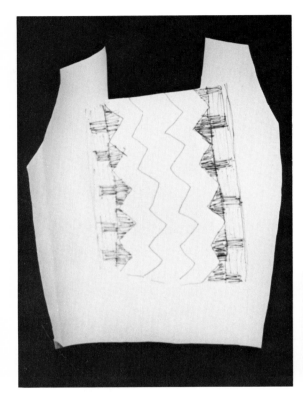

A standard vest pattern was transferred to a large sheet of newsprint paper with the design very loosely sketched in. I purposely left the sides and bottom blank, since as this kind of knitting progresses additional shapes suggest themselves almost automatically.

Here is the front of the vest well under way. The stockinette diagonal strip was done first. The dark brown garter stitch strips were knitted right on, which meant compensating decreases had to be made before and after knitting on at the decrease points. The strips could be knitted separately and stitched together, avoiding the necessity for the extra decreases. The arrows were made like those in the man's vest, on page 185. Two strips of a basket-weave pattern fill out the sides (knit three, purl three, turn and purl three, knit three, for three rows; then reverse the knit-purl pattern). When the back is complete, more strips will be added as needed.

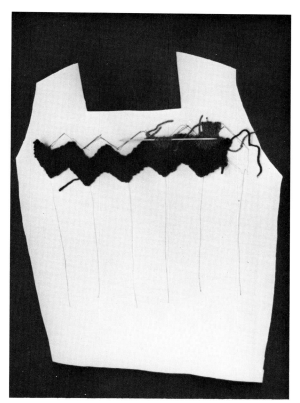

For the back, a diagonal strip is placed horizontally with a row of arrows filled in. Note the use of the small double-pointed needle, which I like to use throughout with this method of knitting. As you can see, the working plan is very sketchy, with the pattern primarily used to control size.

Below, left: The shoulder bands consist of three strips, with the narrow garter bands knit onto the center stockinette one. The little raised cups are knotless netted. The triangles in a row unify the bottom of front and back. They are edged with several rows of single crochets.

Below, right: The back center section is accented with embroidery and knotless netting. The garter stitch sections are knitted horizontally on circular needles, the stitches picked up from the edge of the center band.

Here you see how the sides were filled out with additional knitting. Note the triangle knitted on to shape the armhole. The crochet chain can be laced tightly for a fitted vest look, or left loose for a tabard effect.

The diagonal strip effect can also be achieved with center-out squares as shown in this sketch. This would eliminate the need to fill in the arrow heads, with only the bottoms knitted on as indicated by the dotted lines.

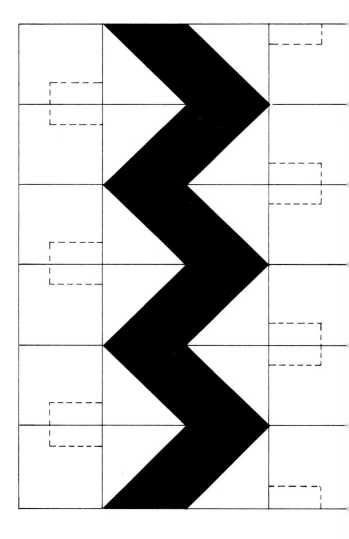

The Colorful Zigzag

In the diagonal strip the bias was created by increasing at one side and decreasing at the other. By decreasing at the beginning and end and making or increasing stitches in the center, a chevron pattern is formed. This too is an integral part of traditional knit technology but, by isolating the pattern into a single repeat on the needle, then attaching individual strips to one another, the overall pattern created permits much more switching around of colors and stitches. The strips are fun and easy to do, and can be used as vertical or horizontal units, individually as well as for large patchworks. Since the beginning and end of the strips dovetail together, they are ideal for tubular projects such as pillows or bags.

To make a zigzag strip, cast on twelve stitches (units can be doubled if desired), knit two together or PSSO, knit three, make a stitch two times, knit three, knit two together or PSSO again. Knit back, then repeat the decrease-knit-increase-knit-decrease pattern. You will have twelve stitches on the needle at the end of each and every row. The zigzag shape emerges after just a few rows.

The strip looks best when colors are switched every few rows. You can also alternate between stockinette and purl stitches. New strips can be sewn, crocheted, or knitted onto previous rows, and this is where the strip method shows off its additional plus feature of allowing variations in the horizontal pattern made by the joined strips. The strips can be used vertically as shown or . . .

. . . joined horizontally. This little drawstring bag was made from the three strips just shown, with the 8½-inch strips folded and sewn horizontally so that the ends dovetail. A narrow knit-sealed tube is used as a drawstring handle, and sewn to the bottom of the bag as a decoration. (See color section, p. 4.)

The Lacy Zigzag

Take the just-described zigzag strip but make the center increases with yarnovers, and watch the strip take on a lacy look. This works out best in a stockinette stitch and with the holes made at either side of the center stitches in each row. Here's how it would work: Cast on twelve, purl twelve to establish a base. Now PSSO, knit three, yarn over, knit two, yarn over, knit three and PSSO for the last two stitches. For the purl row, purl the first two stitches together, purl three, yarn over, purl two, yarn over, purl three and purl two together. Repeat for the length of the strip.

You can accentuate the lacy look in the way you attach the strips: Knit on by attaching to the crossbar that results from the PSSO (every *other* row) as shown in the photo. Yarn over, then turn, and purl two together. This will give you additional little holes or spaces at the join line.

To further open up the lacework, stretch the finished strips to the point of stress. To illustrate, three white acrylic lacy strips were knitted to very barely reach around an orange velour base. The strips for this pillow were stretched very tautly, both vertically and horizontally. A row of single crochet stitches holds everything firmly in place and adds a visually pleasing welting. (See color section, p. 2.)

More Lacy Strip Ideas

Suppose you want a lacelike strip without the zigzag shaping? Old-time pattern books used to publish numerous "receipts" for what was generally referred to as lace insertions. As a rule these were narrow bands, an inch wide at the most and done, like so many things, in white cotton. The patterns given for the lace insertion photos found in the pages of an 1898 *Ladies' World* magazine are the same as the pattern used for the lace curtain hanging in Chapter 6: Yarn over, knit two together, yarn over, knit two together, *on each and every row.* In short, you need three stitches to make the lace, one to knit and two to knit together after the yarnover. A band of twelve stitches would give you four holes to the row.

Lace insertion with knit one, yarn over, knit two together pattern adaptable for a straight lace strip.

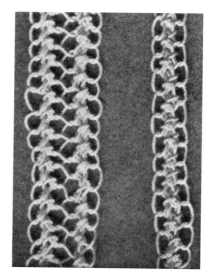

Lace-Fringe Strip

Like everything in creative knitting, one idea leads to another. Suppose you'd like your lace strip to have a fringe. This would certainly be a valuable kind of strip to have available, especially as an edging band. Again, the old pattern books provide an easy solution, essentially the knit-yarnover-knit-two-together band, but with the last three stitches knitted only temporarily. When the band is long enough the last three stitches of each row are unraveled as part of the binding-off process. The following demonstration shows how this works.

Cast on nine stitches and knit, yarn over, knit two together back and forth. When you are ready to end the strip, bind off the first six stitches as shown. Slip the needle out of the remaining three stitches and

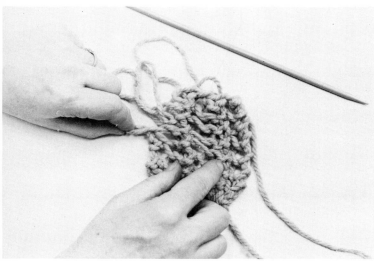

unravel the knitting all the way down the side of the strip. The unraveled stitches form into loops, which could also be cut into open fringes. For a wider band, cast on more stitches, always in units of three. You can also lengthen the loop by unraveling six instead of three stitches.

Lace fringe strip plant hanger.

A Lace-Fringe-Strip Plant Holder

Here's a sample project for the lace-fringe strip that everyone will find useful. Mine was made to fit a small pot. For a larger one, make a wider band with a longer fringe and use plastic cord, raffia, or strong jute instead of rug yarn, which is fine for a small, light pot.

Here's how the illustrated holder is made:

Cast on fifteen stitches, six for the band and nine that will be unraveled into a fringe. Knit one, yarn over and knit two together, back and forth, until the strip fits around the pot. Bind off the six stitches for the band and unravel the rest for a long fringe. Cut the loops open. Fit the band around the pot and bundle the fringe together just where the pot sits. Wrap the fringe securely.

To make the handles, knit on by slipping the needle through three stitches of the band edge. Knit the three stitches in the pattern of the band. Knit to the point where you will want the handles to cross (about five inches). Cut the yarn and put the three stitches on a safety pin or wooden dowel.

Knit a second band, picking up stitches exactly opposite the first one and knit to match.

Put the stitches from the first and second band onto one double-pointed needle, alternating from one to the other. Knit one row with the six stitches on the needle and divide into threes again, putting one trio of stitches on a holder. Knit the three stitches on the needle (the third band) as you did the first and second bands, heading toward the edge of the holder. Pick up three stitches from the edge (in the middle of bands one and two) and alternate these and the three stitches from band three onto one needle. Cut the end of the yarn, thread into an embroidery needle and weave back and forth through the six stitches, securing very firmly. This is, of course, our old friend, the alternate loop attachment.

To complete the hanger, go back to the last three stitches being held and knit the fourth band as you did the third, attaching to the edge of the pot in the same way.

A long hanging band can be knitted out from the point where the four bands cross.

Sara Lane's elegant vest belies the simplicity of its construction. Two straight stockinette bands reach from the front to the back of the fringed lace strip used as a unifying waistband. Sara's bands were not worked horizontally on short needles but vertically on long circular needles—a choice dictated by the yarn, a variegated color yarn that would have produced an unflattering stripe if knitted the short way.

Here Sara combines two NEW LOOK strips, the zigzag and the lacy-strip fringe with a center-out diamond square. If you study the top band and the square for a while you will discover all kinds of possibilities for adding other shapes and enlarging this hanging before adding the final fringe strip.

The Spool Strip

The versatile spool strip begins like a triangle at its widest point, decreased to its tip, and then increased back to its widest point. A long strip of spools can be knitted in garter stitch, lace patterns, or whatever else suits your fancy. The spool is easily widened or narrowed and compatible with numerous other shapes and techniques.

Both these strips are knitted on small needles with a ten-stitch base reduced at the beginning and end of each front-facing row until two stitches are on the needle, then increased back to ten stitches. The lace strip is made by knitting, passing the yarn over, and knitting two together all across. The bottom of the lace strip shows the contrasts possible by knitting on in between the open triangle spaces. The strips can be tacked together with a stitch at the side points with the resulting open diamonds left as negative design areas.

Spool Strip Vest

Six spool strips, three for the front and three for the back, are the basic design units for a figure-flattering vest. When designing a garment with spool strips, it's best to cut some paper patterns of the strips and measure these against a paper garment pattern. That way you can see how wide your strips need to be.

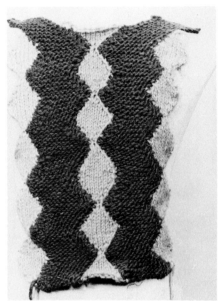

The spool strips are knitted in three different colors, in the stockinette stitch. I knitted the diagonal strips directly in between but they can be worked separately. Note the alignment of the spool strips.

A variegated furlike mohair is knotless netted all around the spools, neckline, waist, and armholes. If I had knitted the diagonal strips separately, I would have crocheted instead of knotless netted and used the crochet as a join as well as a decoration, as in the crocheted garter stitch strip coat shown at the beginning of this chapter. This is actually the better method for this garment, but I was not sure if I wanted to use the "fur" when I began the vest. (See color section, p. 1.)

Garter stitch triangles were knitted in between the spools as a side band.

The original plan called for a full-sleeved sweater, but I found the Icelandic yarn I used, though delightfully soft, was very warm, and decided that a sleeved sweater had best wait for some "cooler" yarn. As you can see from this sketch, the spool strip could be most effectively continued into a sleeve by knitting one strip extending from the shoulder to the wrist. The triangles between the points of the strip would be filled in with garter stitches. A circular needle could be slipped into the invisible cast-off loops of each triangle and the rest of the sleeves knitted in a solid piece. The direction of the lines indicates the direction of the stitches. The zigzag lines show where the sleeve will be seamed.

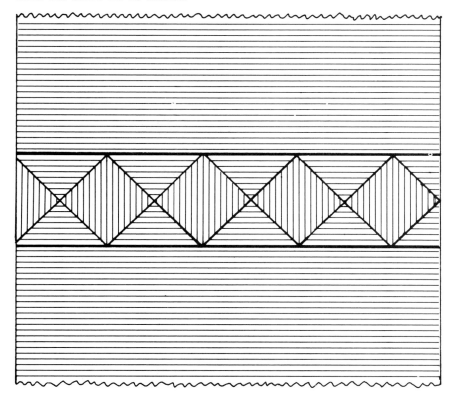

Here's how the sleeve would look when folded and seamed. The strip travels the outside length of the arm. The sleeve is knitted as a straight piece.

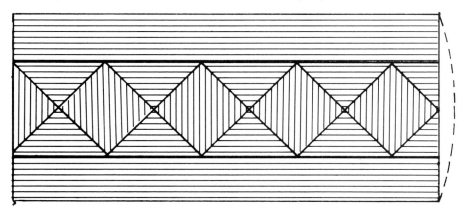

Here's yet another idea for the spool strip. If you hang up stockings at Christmastime, these boots will be enjoyed and remembered long after the goodies stuffed inside are used up. (See color section, p.1.)

Holed leather bases are available from many hobby suppliers or you could fashion your own with the help of soft leather and a hole punch. The spool strip is filled in with garter stitch triangles, which continue on a bias. A row of crochet stitches is worked around the holes of the shoe base. The top of the boot is crocheted together down the back and onto the crochet base of the sole. The boots could also be knitted with more strips as in the vest design on the previous page.

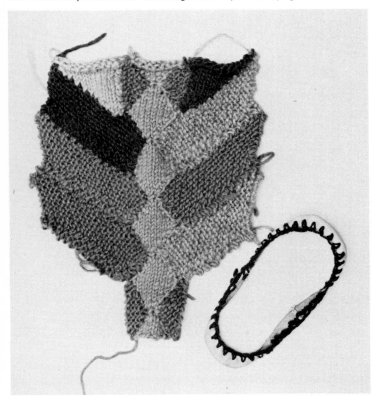

The Knitting Machine as an Art Loom

A chapter devoted to a machine might strike some as paradoxical. Yet its exclusion more than its inclusion would be inconsistent. The machine as a potential art tool is integral to this book's professed purpose of a free and open attitude toward all knitting.

The first knitting machine, like most inventions, came about through one person's search for an easier way of doing something; in this case, the inventor, William Lee, was the husband of an expert and industrious hand knitter. The continued development and sophistication of the machines that have followed that first hosiery knitter have not prevented a burgeoning interest in and appreciation of handcrafted fibers. A number of artists have gone to the machine in an effort to discover a way of knitting that would combine the best that man and machine could produce. The results of some of these experiments have been nothing short of spectacular!

I feel that the time is not far off when loom knit art will be as familiar and accepted a term as fiber sculpture, and when the constantly expanding fiber departments in schools and colleges will be introducing the knitting loom along with that for weaving. Gallery directors like Julie Schaffler and Sandy Lowe have led the way in recognizing and featuring machine knitting. Commissions for machine knit hangings are already a reality.

This chapter is not only a personal appreciation of the artistry possible with this ingenious technological aid but a response to much curiosity expressed by artist friends and acquaintances throughout the country—curiosity thus far unsatisfied because creative and technical education has not been readily available. This then is a first step in filling that gap. Perhaps one day soon there will be an entire book.

To Some the Machine Spells a Whole New Way of Life

Less than five years ago Linda Mendelson's career classification was that of rehabilitation counselor. Today, Linda is a full-time fiber artist and teacher, with the knitting machine her primary medium of self-expression and financial support.

Linda was a good counselor. She was also a good knitter . . . avocationally. When she saw a knitting machine being demonstrated in a neighborhood store she knew that this was something she had to have. She received a rudimentary course with her machine, but her full realization of the machine's scope has come about through personal trial and error. The enthusiasm of her co-workers for the scarves and hats that represented her early effort encouraged Linda sufficiently to embark on more ambitious and artistic types of clothing, to incorporate into her designs her special interest in calligraphy. These calligraphic art garments were an immediate success. Julie's Artisan Gallery in New York sold her first coat within a week of displaying it, for a four-figure sum. More sales, plus private commissions, followed and it was not long before Linda had to make a choice between her first and her new career. She has not regretted opting for the latter for a moment. Her life is so full that she considers her only real problem one of finding time to investigate all the avenues opened for her by her knitting loom. She has made some boutique sweaters and also samples for manufacturers, both of which bring considerable financial rewards. Her art garments continue to sell at impressive prices and these have in turn paved the way for tapestry commissions for offices of corporations. To balance the periods of solitude necessary for working out designs, Linda teaches basic and advanced loom knitting at Threadbare Unlimited, a fiber supply shop and crafts school in New York's Greenwich Village. She took time out from her "live" teaching to clarify some of the procedures and possibilities of loom knitting for our readers. The photographs of Linda and her work are by Charles Decker.

Learning to Loom Knit

Your first question is going to be, what kind of machine shall I get? Since there are so many domestic and foreign brands on the market, it is impossible to recommend one brand. Your choice should follow some thorough consumer orientation on your part, as well as clarifying for yourself as much as possible what your own needs are. One machine might offer special features you'll never use, while another will have something you can't do without. Many machines work best with fine yarns; others take fibers up to rug yarn size. The pros and cons of one machine must be weighed carefully against the other, with the final decision of course dependent on your pocketbook. There are knitting looms to be had for under $200 but some go over $700. There are also the bargain and risk possibilities of buying secondhand. The important thing is to check around, to ask questions.

Threading the Loom

Anyone familiar with a sewing machine and its operations will recognize similarities in the threading procedure.

Meet your teacher, Linda Mendelson, with furry friend.

Two colors are threaded at once, an immediate opportunity for achieving textural variety. Your yarn must be on pull skeins, as shown, or on cones. Some machines take only very fine yarns; Linda's will take anything from fine cotton to regular knitting worsted.

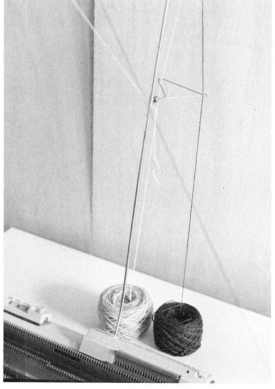

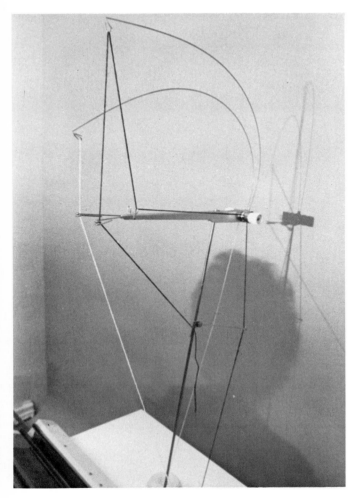

As you study the direction of the threading—from the bottom right, up, over to the left, up and down into the machine—you will recognize the similarity to a sewing machine.

The stitch-control dial is in another way reminiscent of the sewing machine. The little dots in between numbers represent two extra settings so that there are actually thirty stitch sizes from which to choose, not just the ten as marked on the dial.

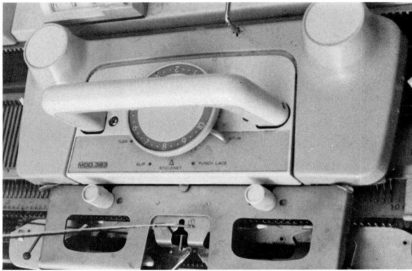

Starting to Knit

Your loom is threaded, and you're ready to proceed. Here's where the difference between hand and machine knitting and machine knitting and the sewing machine comes into play.

Here we see the real difference between hand and loom knitting. The carriage sits atop a bed of needles. When you grip the handle and push the carriage across the needle bed, you make not one but an entire row of stitches. Knitting sixty to ninety rows a minute is far from the realm of possibilities, though this depends on the yarn and pattern used.

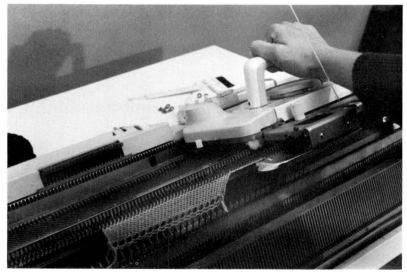

Study this close-up of plain knitting in progress and note that the *wrong side of the work faces you at all times.*

Increasing and Decreasing Stitches

Once you learn to cast on and start knitting, there's one more vital skill to be learned: shaping your work with increases and decreases.

Neither increases nor decreases are hard to master.

To increase, pull forward an extra needle, on either side. When the machine knits, it will automatically knit across this extra needle. Linda is pointing to an extra stitch just made.

Linda uses a transfer tool (one of those little gadgets that are the inevitable accompaniments to all machine purchases) to pull forward a needle and take off a stitch.

This stitch is transferred to another needle with a loop on it. In other words, to decrease you knit two stitches together, exactly as you would in a hand-knit decrease.

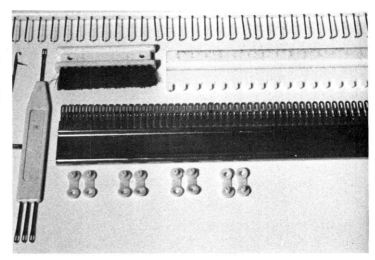

Before going on to pattern knitting, here is an assemblage of some of the extras you are likely to be buying along with your machine: a cast-on comb, a lint brush, a needle pusher, pattern card clips, transfer tools, and a latch hook.

Loom Knit Patterns

While the loom enables you to execute very fine and intricate designs, their planning and execution is not nearly as intricate and mysterious as many machine-shy people assume it to be. The design is drawn onto a special card and punched out. Some manufacturers actually sell pre-punched pattern cards, like painted needlepoint canvases, and it is here that a valid distinction could be made—a distinction based on the approach taken to the machine, the production of an imitative kit type of design or an original one. To facilitate the punching out of the cards, there's another "extra," an automatic puncher.

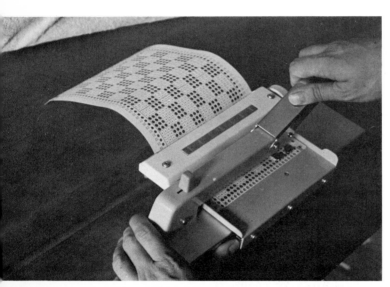

Linda punches out a basic checkerboard pattern with her automatic puncher. This will be incorporated into a cape.

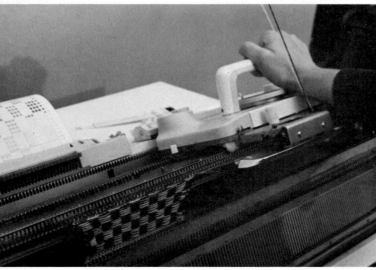

The card is fed into the loom, like paper into a typewriter. The carriage then "reads" the pattern from the card and automatically selects the needles for knitting in dark or light colors.

As with plain machine knitting, the wrong side of the pattern always faces you as the fabric comes off the machine.

The pattern weaves within reach of the loom knitter are virtually infinite. Linda has built up a sizable collection of her weaves and uses them as a reference guide when planning new pieces. The punch cards can be reused.

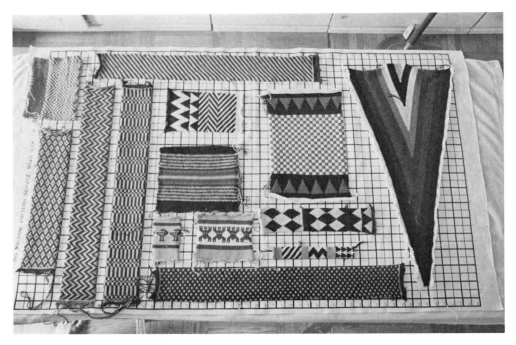

The grid cloth to which these loom knit sketches are pinned is
a special pressing cloth sold in sewing supply stores. Linda finds
this very helpful in blocking her work.

Detail of machine loom weaves.

Another detail.

Machine-loomed Garments

Since knitting looms are limited in terms of the width of the fabric that can be produced, machine-loomed garments are a form of patchwork very much in keeping with the patch strip methods of chapter 9. The strips can be shaped or straight, hand or machine sewn or crocheted together.

The rectangular sleeve used by so many hand knitters is also a favorite with loom artists. Linda makes preliminary sketches for all her garments, using graph paper and a pocket calculator to work out her patterns. The small photo shows the diagram in the lower right-hand corner completed.

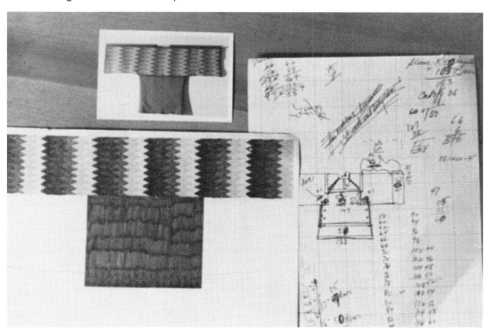

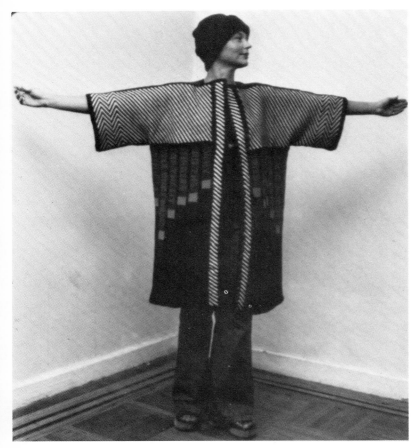

The calligraphy Linda knits into her designs must be set individually, without punch cards. This walking E. E. Cummings poem includes punch-card patterning as well.

The cape with its sweep and drama has never really been out of style, though in recent years its popularity has bordered on being a permanent fad. To the fiber artist a cape is a shaped, functional hanging. The construction is quite simple: long triangles, which when assembled, form a three-quarter circle.

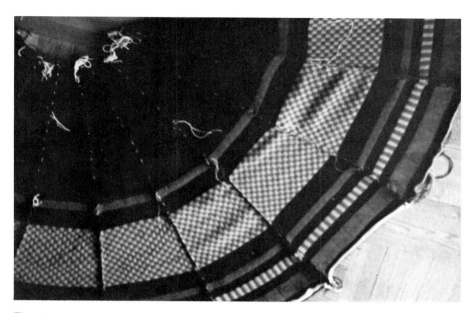

The checked pattern, shown earlier in its planning and progression stages, is seen here as the dominant design of each triangle.

Back view of the finished cape.

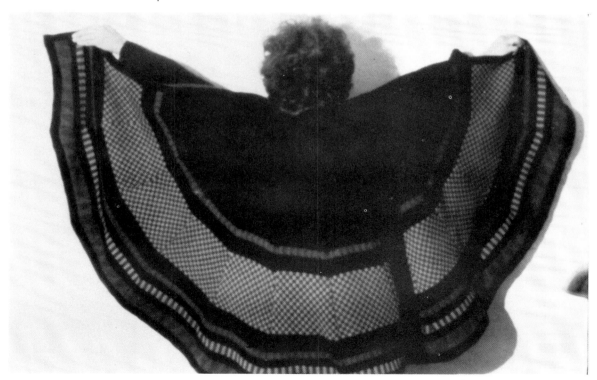

Full front view.

Closed front view.

Accent on Form

Madge Copeland's very first venture into loom knitting should help dispel many fears as to the difficulties of learning to handle the loom with only a minimal knowledge of the technical ins and outs. Her method of utilizing the loom should be of special interest to those more interested in form and shape than surface design patterns.

When we told Madge, a frequent contributor to past fiber books, about this venture into creative knitting, she toyed with the idea of reactivating her hand-knitting skills, but opted instead to try the machine loom as an alternative to her large "regular" one. An advertisement in the local paper, stating her desire to buy or rent a used machine, brought Madge in contact with Jennie Schnaitman, who learned to master her machine completely alone, years earlier. Mrs. Schnaitman's personalized machine-knit hats and sweaters have been a source of income, both from local stores and private customers. She agreed to show Madge how to cast on, increase and decrease, and let her try her luck. The machine is now a permanent fixture in the Copeland studio.

If Madge had knitted her tube on Linda Mendelson's loom, she would have had to seam it since a single-bed machine (Linda's) has the capability to produce only very narrow tubes formed by the natural curl of the fabric, but not really sealed. The machine Madge used, however, had a double bed of needles and by using both of these, it was possible to produce a seamless tube. Though there was no design patterning, the artist did introduce a lovely pattern of colors by moving from bright orange to magenta to shiny red. Decreases and increases were geared around color changes. Since traditional weaving, which has been Madge's main medium, has little stretch, the twenty-foot length of the finished hanging is admittedly something of an unplanned surprise. The topsy-like growth has served to put Madge on her guard in anticipation of the stretch factor.

The rings that help define and support the shape of the space hanging were inserted after the knitting was complete. The shiny red portion of the tube was pulled inside the orange and magenta section, and this tube-within-a-tube with one color shimmering through the others, is very dramatic. Keith Brewster photographed the tube when it was hung from a tree in the Copeland backyard, though it moved to a gallery shortly thereafter.

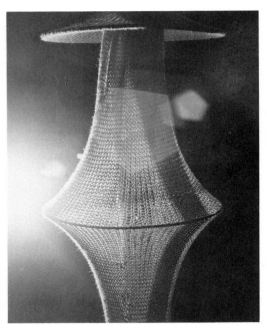

The look of the knitting can be varied depending on the diameter of the rings, as is evident in this close-up view.

The hanging is completely collapsible, which makes it easy to transport and, if necessary, to store.

Jenny Schnaitman's perky ski hat shows the versatility of the knitting loom in creating both functional and nonfunctional items.

For those readers who like the space-hanging form but have neither access to nor the inclination for loom knitting, here is yet another knitted space hanging—this one was made on that most rudimentary of "machines," the rake (see chapter 2), by Linda Hendricks.

Top, right: The holes in the hanging were created by looping back and forth instead of all around some of the areas.

Bottom: Another view of Linda Hendricks's rake knitted space hanging.

Mary Ann Mauro combines machine knitting with a potpourri of other fiber techniques.

Detail of Mary Ann Mauro's "Night Music."

Quilt Art, "Painted" on the Knitting Loom

Susanna Lewis, like Linda Mendelson, is an experienced and expert hand knitter. For several years she enjoyed considerable success with appliqué and quilt commissions, but she wanted to broaden her artistic endeavors. Weaving beckoned, but Susanna yearned for something with weaving's challenge, plus a chance to tread virgin territory as an artist. A happenstance walk past the Pfaff showroom provided the answer to her quest.

The knitting loom has enabled Susanna to combine both her quilting and appliqué skills and her love and knowledge of nature. The resulting work has that immediately identifiable uniqueness that every artist hopes to achieve. It truly defies any association with words such as commercial or industrial. As for acceptance of the work, Susanna has found a ready outlet for her knit art through private commissions and gallery shows ("some juried shows still reject anything labeled as being machine knit"). Susanna finds the restraints imposed by a client's space and personal interests challenging rather than hampering. She also believes that people who buy her work do have a right to be concerned about its care and cleaning and this is one of the reasons she works almost exclusively with acrylics. Her quilt backings are all completely washable and Susanna assured us that any of her hangings could actually be washed like anyone's delicate laundry. Perhaps the fact that her own home and studio is in Brooklyn's Park Slope, an area rich in splendid examples of handsome brownstone houses but equally rich in dust and soot, has underlined the need for creating easily maintained fiber art.

Susanna's designs are carefully planned on graph paper, with much of the patterning developed right in the machine, from row to row.

"Roses" was knitted with acrylic yarns and appliquéd. It measures 52" by 39".

Sketch for a shell hanging.

Note the correlation of the design and contour of the appliqued shells and background. 51″ by 55″.

Once again the central motif is part of an overall design. Perhaps you will recognize the butterfly background as being in the shape of the moth larva.

This mixed media quilt of machine knitting and appliqué is reminiscent of the shell hanging, though it makes a totally new statement. (See color section, p. 1.)

Again we see a motif repeated, first as a hanging . . .

and very differently, as a coat.

Her involvement with the knitting loom has expanded Susanna's interest in clothing. Coats like this wonderful knitted fairy tale are sold through galleries like Julie's Artisan Gallery.

The construction is one of hand-sewn patch strips and straight sleeves.

11
Mergers: Multimethod and Mixed-Media Ideas

In a book like this there are always some ideas that defy organizational categories, and others which seem to demand a special time and place of their own. This chapter embodies that special time and place and recapitulates for the reader techniques taught earlier in a somewhat larger perspective. The mixed-media knittings illustrate the interaction possible between knitting and other crafts, when the approach is open-minded. This then is a visual restatement of the philosophy behind this book, that knitting can be planned and orderly, or spontaneous; a fun craft or an art craft.

The following knit hanging is part of a series of fiber patchworks, combining circular and geometric forms, letting the design grow organically, shape by shape. The first of these hangings was done as a commission for a crochet fan. As I became more and more involved in knitting I realized that the validity of what I wanted to do in this medium rested on my learning to create forms I had previously crocheted. As the knit shapes grew and grew so, happily, did my enthusiasm. The knit hanging was in many ways much more successful than its crochet predecessor. Most importantly, it was a pleasure and a joy to create. The methods for making ruffles and creating trapunto effects were borne out of this effort, along with a greater intimacy with the circle and its variations and the technique for knitting on. Instructions for methods used can be found in earlier chapters and will not be described here.

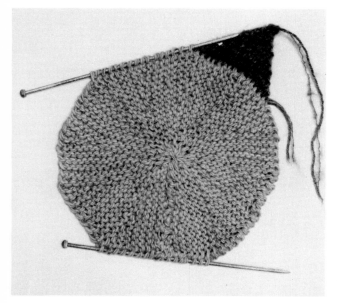

It all began with a ten-inch-diameter garter stitch circle. To start the organic growth, two triangles were knitted on at the top of the circle, and one large one at the bottom. Needles were inserted directly into the edge of the circle. The short triangles were increased at the beginning and end of every stockinette row; the longer triangle was increased only every other stockinette row.

A few rows of straight knitting were added at the top of the small triangles to provide an even base for the addition of the next shape: a square knitted all in one piece, with the center diamond formed by carrying an extra color. The shape could also have been made with four small center-out squares or one large center-out diamond patch.

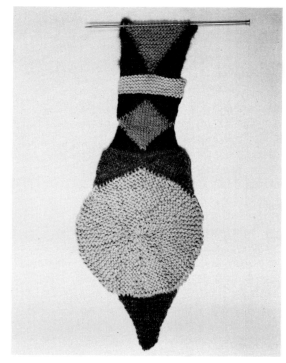

After a few rows of straight garter stitches, two triangles decreased on the diagonal were added. The garter stitch section was knitted on in between these triangles.

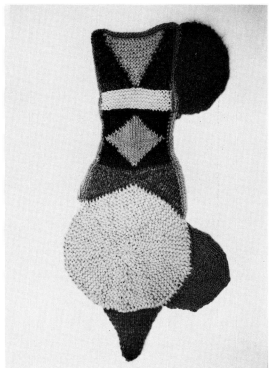

Wherever a narrow outline was needed before adding a new shape, one or two rows of single crochet stitches were added. After the first such crochet outlining, several half circles were knitted separately and attached with crochet slip stitches. The shapes were diversified by means of alternating between garter and stockinette stitches and of course through the use of different colors and textures as you can see when referring to the color section.

The half circles at the right were balanced by adding identical ones at the other side. The gaps in between the top and bottom circular forms were filled in by picking up stitches from the side and knitting on at the edge of the circles. The circular needle was left in the stitches since the shapes were continued in a striped pattern.

Here we see three stripes filled in at each side. These were done in three parts, knitting straight up for the center sections and then knitting the side pieces up and on. The attachment of these side-to-center pieces automatically increased the shape. The bottom triangle was also extended with stripes. These were worked on three double-pointed needles, with an extra stitch made at each side of the point to keep the shape defined. The top part of the stripe surrounding the triangle was knitted onto the bottom of the half circles. Two rows of single crochets edge everything done so far.

More additions were made at the bottom. A garter stitch circle was knitted separately and fitted around the triangle instead of being closed.

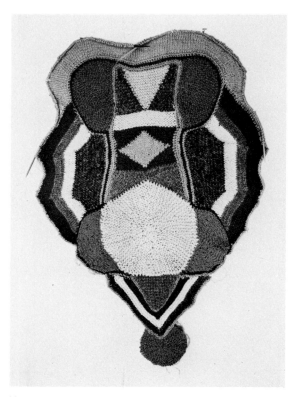

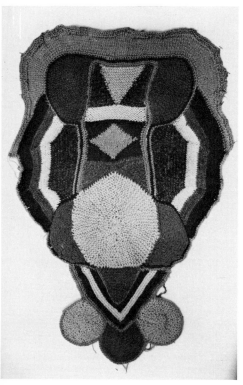

Here is the bottom circle slip-stitched in place and a large section of stockinette stitch knitting added all around the top. Two circular needles were used as one as can be seen in the picture. Increases were made around the curves to keep the overall shape flat.

Two additional garter stitch circles, this time closed, round things out at the bottom, and once again an edging of crochet is worked all around.

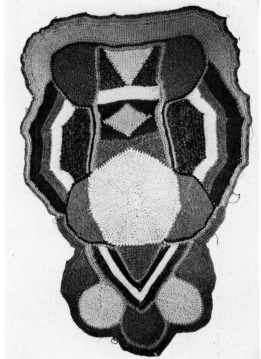

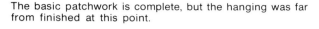

The basic patchwork is complete, but the hanging was far from finished at this point.

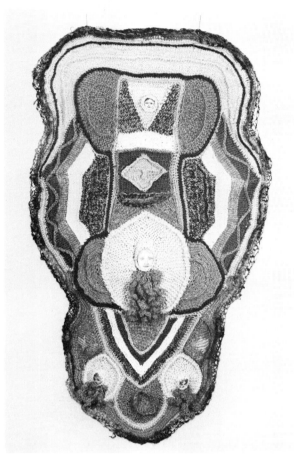

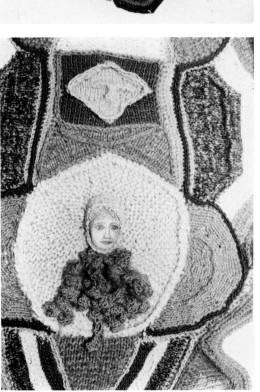

Adding surface details is half the fun.

I usually start things off by finding some place for the ink-drawn stones that are my special love. The four in this hanging are encased in little pockets of knotless netting. Knotless netting was also used for the variegated mohair border.

The trapunto method was used for the face of the square just above the central circle, and to accentuate the tweedy section of the striped areas at the side with a geometric mock-cable design. Meandering single crochet stitches were added to the last stripe at each side.

The collarlike ruffles of three of the stones are made with a mixture of cowhair and mohair, a blending used in several other areas.

The arrows at either side of the bottom triangle are embroidered on top of the stockinette surface. (See color section, p. 2.)

Close-up view of some of the finishing details.

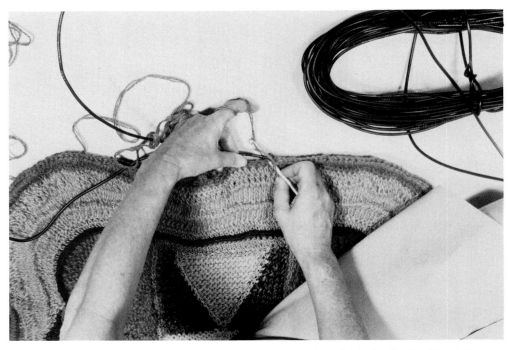

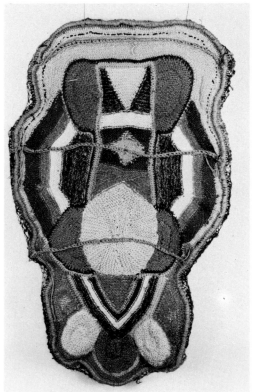

In a hanging of this size (2½′ by 4′) it is important to plan how the piece will hang. Since this hanging was made in what, at least to me, was the shape of a large shield, I decided to emphasize the shield effect in the mounting. Heavy, plastic-coated wire was covered and attached all around with single crochet stitches.

Two additional crochet-covered plastic-coated wire bands were attached across the back, and if you look closely at the finished hanging, you will note how these extra bands were manipulated to make the surface of the hanging at once concave and convex.

A Playful Blanket

Translating three popular board games into a knitted blanket offered an opportunity to play around with five knitting techniques: Triangles in a row, color stranded patch strips, garter stitch circles squared off with triangles, crochet patched garter stitch strips, and outside-in squares.

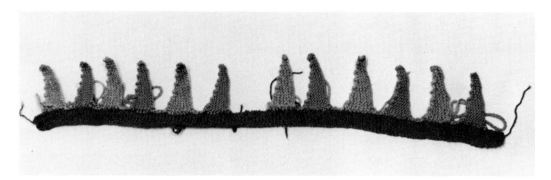

The idea and design for the blanket started with the backgammon game. The first step was to work out the arithmetic for the playing triangles. The long strip onto which points would be added was made vertically, just six stitches on the needle. The long triangles were knitted on all in a row. Eleven stitches were cast on for each triangle, and each triangle was decreased two stitches at a time (one PSSO and one knit two together). Two strips like this had to be made. (See directions for the star in chapter 8, and triangles in a row, chapter 9.)

The triangles to be fitted in between the game points were made by knitting onto a wide strip on either side. This wide strip would serve as the center of the board. Little effort was made to attach the points very smoothly since a raised crochet stitch divider line was part of the overall plan.

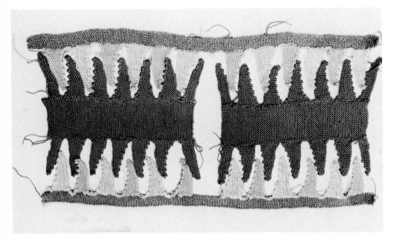

Here is the basic game, ready to be connected. Single crochet stitches were used to connect and outline the game points. A garter stitch strip was knitted in between the two play areas.

The checkerboard was knitted in strips of two boxes each, carrying the colors from one square to the next. The borders were knitted on, two facing sides at a time.

The ticktacktoe game was patched together by first making nine garter stitch circles and squaring these off by knitting triangles all around, as one would knit triangles in a row (compare this to the way the central cicle of the previously illustrated hanging was squared off.)

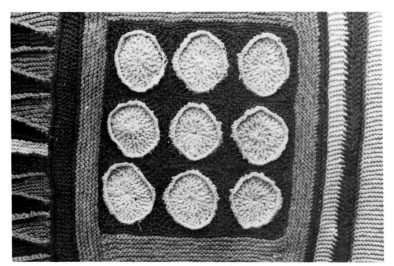

The squared-off circles were patched into strips of three, which were in turn patched into a square and bordered in garter stitch, as in the checkerboard.

Once the three games were patched together, the blanket continued to grow. The border strips were all separately knitted and patch-crocheted in place. Sixteen outside-in squares were interspersed around the last border strips. (See color section, p. 7.)

A Stockinette "Canvas" Surrounded by *NEW LOOK* Shapes

Our friendship with Sara Lane took shape along with the shaping techniques for this book. Sara was one of the first artists to give me her reactions to the various center-out shapes and the over-all concept of knitting on. Her contributions to this book are manifold and this lovely 62-by-84-inch hanging is the culmination of her enthusiasm.

The embroidered flower is the focus of the hanging, surrounded by a patchwork of knit-on shapes.

This numbered diagram shows the progression of the various design areas.

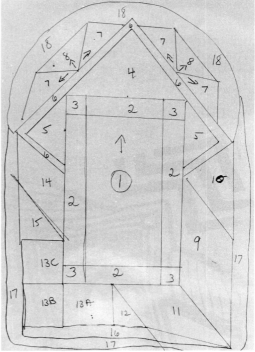

The stockinette canvas measures 21″ by 32″. Sara originally planned to do cross-stitch embroidery but found crochet slip-stitching allowed her more freedom. The center of the flower is a series of French knots.

The striped borders (#2 on diagram) are knitted on separately on long circular needles. The corners are center-in-out squares in two colors.

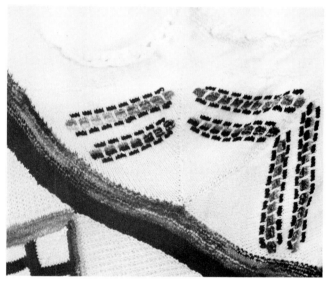

The #4 and #5 triangles were knitted on in a knit one, purl one rib stitch, and this triptych unit was worked by first knitting on the #7 triangles and then knitting the #8 unit in between. The diagram arrows indicate the direction of the stitches. Note the effective use of small areas of multicolored mohair yarn as accents and unifiers throughout.

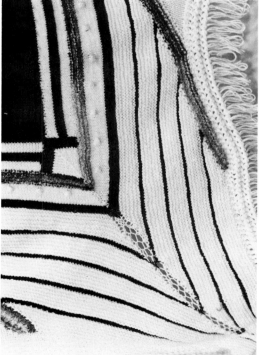

The bottom right-hand corners were made with two diagonal units. The #10 triangle in the diagram is a fill-in area.

The lower left-hand corner consists of three very large center-in-out squares. The #12 shape on the diagram was another fill-in area. For her final shape, #14 in the diagram, Sara repeated the diagonal theme, with #15 another fill-in area. The area marked 16 in the diagram was a fill-in to even out the bottom. The freewheeling irregularity of the piece was completed with two different kinds of borders (#17 and #18). The #18 border was done in a ripple effect (like our first project in chapter 3) and a crochet edging. The #17 border is a long lacy fringe band sewn on. For greater portability while working, all shapes could have been knitted separately and sewn together when everything was done.

Here embroidery is combined with knitting in a collaborative effort. The flower tree trunk and base are knitted by Nancy Lipe—popcorn stitches for the trunk and lacy knitting stretched over a pillow for the base. The flowers were made by Pat Bliss—crewel embroidery on fabric. Nancy and Dewey Lipe are the owners of this unusual nature study.

Painted and Printed Knitting

Here's an alternative to the tapestry method of incorporating color and design into knitting. Since yarns are dyed, why not apply the color after the yarn has been knitted? Dori Graepel, who experimented with this method especially for this book, used free-form brush painting and that simplest of all hand printers, the carved potato. Dori worked with acrylic paints that require no "setting" for permanence and washability and recommends linen as her own favorite yarn for this combination. For those who want to use wool or acrylic for their canvases, I would suggest substituting fabric or textile dyes for the acrylic paint and setting the colors by pressing with a hot steam iron.

The delicate leaves and branches were hand painted on the stockinette circle. The pillow is knitted all in one piece, using alternating knit and purl stitch patterning as described at the beginning of chapter 6.

The owls on this all-stockinette pillow were printed with a hand-carved potato printer. The leaves are hand painted. The owl at the left has mirror eyes.

Dori again makes stockinette inserts within mostly garter stitch knitting. The design is hand painted with acrylic paints.

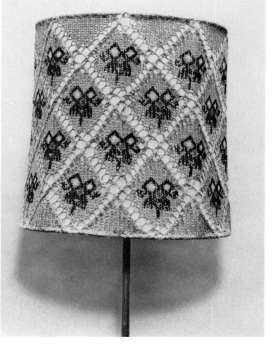

Here we see a classic diamond lace pattern knitted on circular needles, with the owl motifs stamped out from another potato printer. All of Dori's painted and printed knittings, except this lampshade, can be seen in the color section.

Knit Crochet

The yarns you used for your knitting greatly influence the feeling and success of the finished product. Handspun and hand-dyed fiber have their own special beauty and intimacy. A large bag of assorted hand-dyed and unspun fleece and fleece roving inspired this idea for using the crochet hook to do the job of a spindle.

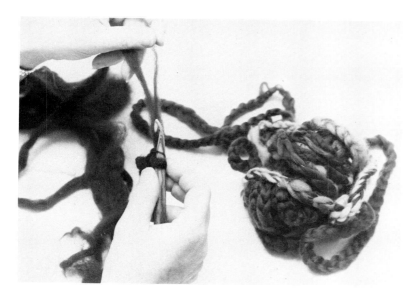

The fleece is twisted as for spinning and crocheted into a chain. As you use up a piece of twisted fleece, lay in a new piece. By using different colors and thicknesses you will be crochet-spinning your own thick and thin variegated yarns.

The yarn crochet spun in the previous picture is knitted into a garter stitch rectangle to serve as a trunk for this pillow. The blending of the crochet chain and the knitting results in an interesting surface, more akin to weaving than knitting. The leaves of the tree are knitted cowhair ruffles. The sky is a large garter stitch circle of blue and white crochet spun fleece. The circle is folded in half, stuffed and stitched. The sun is made of two small yellow half circles. The foliage on this side of the pillow is in fall colors, the back is in summer greens. (See color section, p. 8.)

The method of crochet spinning can be adapted to the use of leftovers. Cut yarns into lengths, sort to allow for a variegated pattern, and crochet into a chain of yarn. To tie the ends of one chain to another, make a weaver's knot as shown in the photograph and cut the ends close to the knot. The blending pattern of the yarn will determine how best to use your yarn for knitting. The sample yarn was made with very short lengths of rainbow colors so that it seemed best to work it into a narrow knit band or tube.

The knitted stockinette tube was sewn all around a small hula-hoop and the leftovers knit into the hoop in a random and abstract pattern of lace stitches.

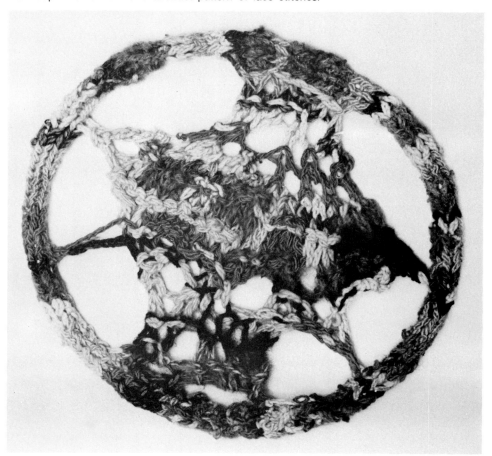

More Media Mergers

Coiling, weaving, macramé, and fabric art—these are just a few of the additional ways in which knitting can be merged with other media.

B. Joan Langley's "King Corn Form" was derived from a play about the Mound Builders of Ohio and Indiana, which she had seen on television. The culture of these Indians was based on the cultivation of maize, and so the artist coiled a raffia basket, to which she added the coblike configurations, also of raffia. These were knitted with the reverse of the stockinette stitch showing. Each was constructed on four needles, from the base to the point. Additional loose raffia was stuffed inside each finger.

Detail view of the cornlike surface of the knitting.

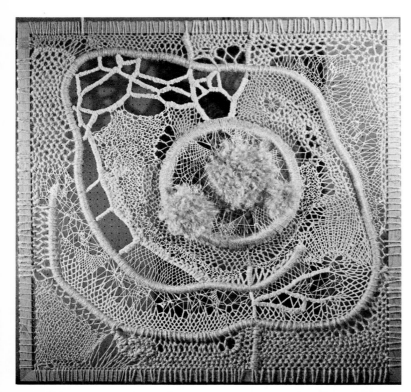

See if you can pick out the knitted areas in this collage of fiber techniques and materials by Evelyn Svec Ward. Photo by William E. Ward.

Nancy and Dewey Lipe joined forces to execute this truly incredible Christmas tree which combines macramé, crochet, and knitting. A wooden post, wire, and wire netting support the seven-foot-tall, five-foot-wide construction.

The body of Robin Gudehus's jacket was woven. The sleeves and collar are knitted.

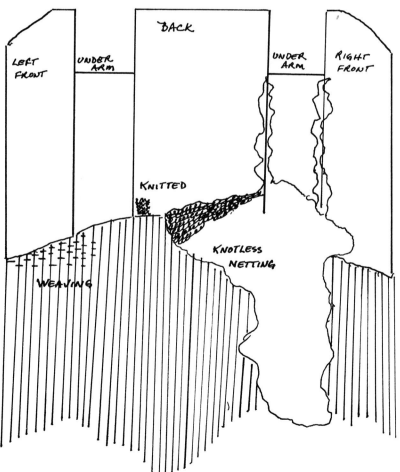

This is Yvonne Porcella's original plan sketch for a knitted, woven, and knotless netted coat. See color section.

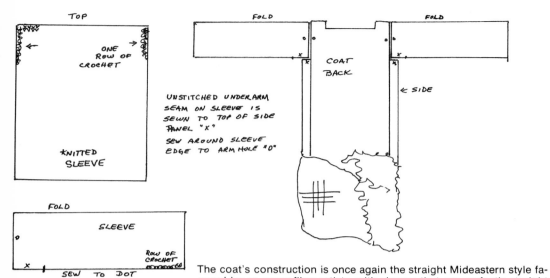

TOP

← ONE ROW OF CROCHET →

KNITTED SLEEVE

FOLD

SLEEVE

ROW OF CROCHET

SEW TO DOT

FOLD   FOLD

COAT BACK

← SIDE

UNSTITCHED UNDER ARM
SEAM ON SLEEVE IS
SEWN TO TOP OF SIDE
PANEL "X"
SEW AROUND SLEEVE
EDGE TO ARM HOLE "0"

The coat's construction is once again the straight Mideastern style favored by so many fiber artists, with sleeves that are perfectly straight rectangles.

The body of the coat is knitted and pinned to a pressboard. The knotless netting areas are made separately and sewn in place. Warps are tied to the knitted and netted edges for the waving.

Here is the weaving progressing. The artist had to allow for the different properties of each of her techniques. Weaving has no stretch, knotless netting a little, and knitting a lot, so Yvonne deliberately made her knitted panels small to compensate for any discrepancies.

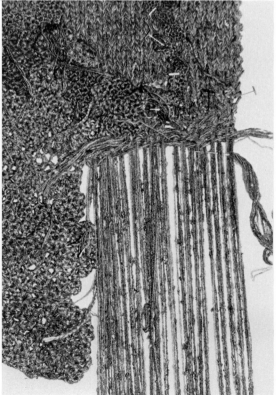

Here is the finished coat being modeled by Suzanne Porcella. Note the wrapped details at the front. (See color section p. 6.)

Detail view of the knotless netted closure.

Back view of the coat. Note how the knotless netting has been used to cover the seam. The coat is a mixture of thin and slubbed wool and rayon yarns, dyed by Maggie Brosnan, in rich shades of purple and rust.

Above: Areas of knitting work well with a mostly fabric quilt by Mary Ann Scarborough. Photo by Sally Davidson. (See color section, p. 8.)

Above, right: Detail of the knitted areas of the crazy quilt.

Nancy and Dewey Lipe like the combination of sumptuous fabrics with fibers—to wit, this sculpture of velvet and knitted tubes, plus knitted ruffles and drawstring balls.

Can you identify the knitting in this sculptural assemblage of knitting, macramé, rya knotting, crewel, and sewing? By Nancy and Dewey Lipe.

There is no end to the sensuously elegant mixed media forms possible when designed and executed by the talented Lipes.

Knitting and Fun *Do* Mix

We'd like to leave readers with some things that epitomize the fun and fantasy spirit that seems to have been a missing link in the story of knitting. These final projects prove once again that you don't have to venture into enormous undertakings to experience the pleasure of creating in a more offbeat and sculptural vein.

Nancy Lipe's pattern sewn teddy gains a distinctive "Nancy-like" personality with a sweater of bouncy knit balls.

Another pattern sewn toy, seems to actually look happier with a shell knitted in NEW LOOK techniques.

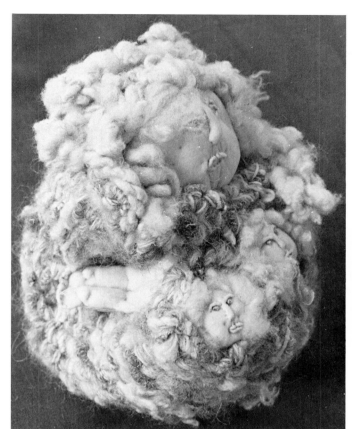

Finally, who can resist Yvonne Porcella's delightful doll containers knitted with unspun fibers and humanized with stuffed stocking doll faces.

"Snow Lady" measures just 7″ by 8″. Cotton-waste handspun in Mexico is knitted on #15 needles with random increases and decreases, with crochet joins.

This last container reminds us of what a famous comedian once said, "Leave them laughing." So laugh and enjoy, for knitting *is* indeed fun!

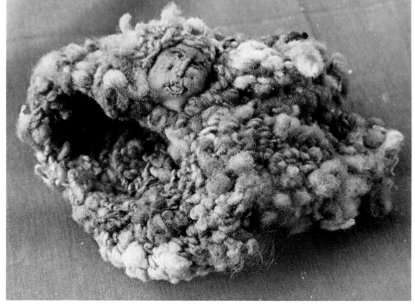

Glossary of Standard Knitting Terms and Abbreviations

Creative knitting encourages a nonregimented, self-starting approach. There will be times when you will want to use patterns or parts thereof. Following are some of the most common terms and abbreviations you will encounter.

K St.—knit stitch. This always refers to the basic knit stitch made by inserting the needle into the front of the loop and bringing yarn under and over needle.

P St.—purl stitch. This is the second basic stitch in all knitting, made by holding yarn in front and inserting needle from back to front of stitch, bringing yarn over and under. Also known as the reverse stockinette stitch.

St. St.—stockinette stitch. When using knit stitch on one row and purl stitch on returning row, the knit stitch row or smooth face of the fabric is identified as stockinette stitch knitting.

K 1 b—knit one stitch in back loop. This is also known as the Continental stitch, a variation of the basic knit stitch, made by inserting the needle in the back of the loop rather than front; less stretchy than regular knit stitch.

P 1 b—same as K 1 b, except that you are purling.

YO—yarnover. Every stitch involves wrapping yarn around needle. Unless otherwise indicated, you make one yarnover per stitch. A yarnover in between stitches, not as part of a regular stitch, creates a space.

G St.—garter stitch. This is the stitch produced by knitting *every* row.

Sl—slip, as to slip a stitch without knitting.

Sl 1 st. pw—slip a stitch purlwise; in other words, slip a stitch as if you were going to purl, but don't purl.

Wl.—wool.

Wl. fwd.—bring wool forward.

Wl.bk—wool in back.

Co—cast on as to cast on first set of stitches.

Bo—bind off. Bound-off stitches have a selvaged edge made by knitting together two stitches and slipping the first over the second.

Rnd—round, as in circular knitting.

Dpn—double-pointed needles.

Dec—decrease. Unless otherwise specified, dec is made by knitting two stitches together.

PSSO—pass slip stitch over. An alternative decrease method. Slip a stitch, knit the next, and pass the slipped stitch over the knit stitch. Pattern might read s.1, k.1, PSSO which translates into slip one, knit one, pass slipped stitch over the knit stitch.

Inc—increase. Unless another method is indicated, inc by knitting into the front and back of the same stitch.

M 1—make one. Same as inc.

O—over. This is an increase made by bringing yarn over after stitch is complete and before new one is started. This creates an increase with a space.

02—over two times.

Pat.St.—pattern stitch. This refers to the group of stitches needed to complete a pattern. The pat.sts. are set off by asterisks.

Gauge—this is the key used in pattern instructions to indicate the number of stitches and rows that equal an inch with the yarn and needles to be used. To check your gauge against that given in pattern, knit a small swatch using needles and the predominant stitch pattern. If pattern gauge states 5 sts. equal 1 inch and 5 rows equal 1 inch, and your swatch does not match this, tighten up your knitting by using thinner needles or thinner yarn and conversely switch to fatter needles or fatter yarn if your swatch is smaller than indicated by the gauge. If you prefer not to switch yarn or needles, use fewer or more stitches until your knitting matches the indicated gauge.

"A New Look at Knitting" Glossary of Terms and Techniques

Some of the methods are unique to this book with its especially coined terminology. Some, like the invisible cast-on-off, grafting, and stranding, are historically established techniques. Their newness lies in the focus and direction. Photographic demonstrations and illustrations pertaining to everything listed here may be found by checking the index.

Invisible Cast-On—method of casting on stitches without a selvage. Length of yarn is held alongside needle with the loops wrapped around the thread and needle. Needles can be reinserted into loops for additional knitting; loops can be finished with crochet, knotless netting, or by tying in fringes.

Invisible Cast-Off—instead of binding off stitches, end yarn is threaded through loops on needle. As with invisible cast-on, there are numerous options for securing or continuing onward with this type of ending.

Invisible Cast-On-Off—above method.

Alternate Loop Join—two pieces of knitting are joined by placing invisible cast-on-off loops on one needle, in alternate order, pulling end yarn of knitting through all stitches. To firmly secure join, weave yarn from other end through in opposite direction.

Alternate Loop Attachment—same as above except that second set of loops are picked up from surface or edge of finished knitting.

251

Knitting On—knitting one piece directly to another by picking up stitch or stitches from edge, top, bottom, or surface. When no increase is desired, the picked-up stitch must be preceded or followed by a decrease.

Knit-Sealed tube—tube made by knitting on double-pointed needles without turning work. Tubes will have a stockinette face. Technique will not work with more than six to eight stitches.

Knit Coiling—knit-sealed tubes formed into flat or three-dimensional coiled forms, joining the coil by knitting on as the work progresses rather than stitching into shape when finished.

Mock Cables—knit-sealed tubes appliquéd for cable effects. Unlike "conventional" cables, these can be multicolored.

Trapunto—using needle and yarn to raise up areas of a knit surface to add texture and stability. An effect that combines look of embroidery and cabling.

Ruffles—knitted ruffles created by contracting groups of stitches. Intensive decreasing is followed by casting on additional stitches. Continuous decrease-cast-on knitting causes fabric to spiral and curl.

Leaves—variations of the ruffle, with shape ended with very abrupt casting off.

Drawstring Balls—spherical forms using invisible cast-on-off, straight knitting. Cast-on-off ends are pulled drawstring fashion to form the sphere.

Garter Stitch Circle—flat circle made by knitting twelve segments, each in a series of short or incomplete rows.

Sizing Pattern—a freer approach to knitting accurately fitting garments than the stitch and row gauge keys used in conventional patterns. Use a paper pattern for front, back, sleeves of garment (or old sweater cut apart or dressmaking patterns), using method detailed in chapter 4 to arrive at accurate dimensions, and keep holding knitting against pattern, increasing or decreasing as needed to stay within the outlines of the pattern. These life-sized patterns can also be used for estimating size of patches or strips, planning tapestry designs, serving as combination size and design-sketch pattern.

Stockinette Stitch Circle—same as garter stitch circle, using only ten segments.

Garter Stitch or Stockinette Stitch Spheres—spheres made like garter and stockinette stitch circles, but with short row patterning at each end of the segments. Can also be used to form drapes for hangings.

Sectional Knitting—dividing stitches to knit separately, rejoining as desired.

Knitting Loom—alternative name for knitting machine.

Stranding or Weaving In—tapestry method of weaving in colors of yarn not in use at the back of the fabric. Equally useful whenever yarn is changed or work is sectioned off and rejoined.

Grafting—invisible method for joining pieces of knitting by grafting on an extra row of stitches. An established method that has new significance for knitting patchwork circles and patchwork joining in general.

Cast-On-Bind-Off Method—moving from one end to another of a knitted base without actually knitting, by binding off stitches. By leaving one loop on needle, the knitting can be formed into a circle, or knitted shapes can be added on by casting on additional stitches.

Triangles-in-a-Row—method of knitting triangular shapes (or rectangles or squares) onto a base and binding off toward the base when the shape is complete.

Printed Knitting—imprinting designs from a stamp (i.e., potato printer) onto stockinette knit surface; an alternative to knitting in designs or tapestry knitting.

Painted Knitting—same as printed knitting, but using a brush.

Fancy Stitch Definitions—condensed and simplified:

Bell—a detached triangle.

Cable—an attached braid.

Lace Knitting—holemaking.

Bibliography

De Dillmont, Therese. *Encyclopedia of Needlework.* Millhause, France, Facsimile edition, Philadelphia, Pa.: Running Press, Inc., 1972.

Kiewe, Heinz Edgar. *The Sacred History of Knitting.* Oxford, England: Art Needlework Industries Ltd., 1967.

McKim, Ruby. *101 Patchwork Patterns.* New York: Dover Publications, 1962.

Mon Tricot. *Knitting Dictionary: Stitches and Patterns.* New York: Crown Publishers, 1973.

Norbury, James. *Traditional Knitting Patterns.* New York: Dover Publications, 1972.

Phillips, Mary Walker. *Creative Knitting.* New York: Van Nostrand Reinhold Co., 1971.

Sommer, Elyse. *A Patchwork, Appliqué and Quilting Primer.* New York: Lothrop Lee and Shepard Co., 1975.

———. *Inventive Fiber Crafts.* Englewood Cliffs, N.J.: Prentice-Hall, Inc., 1976.

Sommer, Elyse and Mike. *A New Look at Crochet.* New York: Crown Publishers, 1975.

Thomas, Mary. *Mary Thomas's Book of Knitting Patterns.* New York: Dover Publications, 1972.

———. *Mary Thomas's Knitting Book.* New York: Dover Publications, 1972.

Walker, Barbara. *A Treasury of Knitting Patterns.* New York: Charles Scribner's Sons, 1968.

———. *The Craft of Lace Knitting.* New York: Charles Scribner's Sons, 1971.

Sources of Supplies

The supplies needed for knitting are easily obtained from local yarn shops and novelty and department stores. To make your knitting more interesting, investigate cords and ropes in hardware stores and yarns sold in stores catering to weavers and fiber people generally rather than knitters and crocheters only. Since the specialty supplier is not as readily located, especially by those living in a small town, the following list of those who supply yarns (as well as beads, feathers, and often books) by mail is included. This list is by no means all-inclusive, nor is inclusion tantamount to a personal endorsement. Where no price for samples and catalogues is given, it is suggested that you send a #10, stamped self-addressed envelope with your inquiries.

Broadway Yarns—Cascade Fiber Co.
P. O. Box 1350
Sanford, N.C. 27330

Polyester yarns and cords in heathery colors. $1 for color card, $3 for color card one 4-ounce skein

William Condon & Sons
65 Queen St.
Charlottetown, P.E.I., Canada

Contessa Yarns
Box 37
Lebanon, Conn. 06247

Novelty yarns

255

Coulter Studios 118 East 59 St. New York, N.Y. 10022	Imported and domestic yarns, weaving and other needlework equipment, dyes, books
Crafts Kaleidoscope 6551 Ferguson St. Indianapolis, Ind. 46220	Cords, yarns, beads, books
Dharma Trading Co. P. O. Box 1288 Berkeley, Calif. 94701	Yarns, cords, dyes. Samples, 75 cents
Fallbrook House Country Arts 480 Canton St. Troy, Pa. 96974	Yarns, spinning supplies, feathers, books
Folklorico Box 625 Palo Alto, Calif. 94302	Their own yarns plus domestics and imports, dyes, beads, books. Catalogue and samples 75 cents
Greentree Ranch Wools 163 N. Carter Lake Rd. Loveland, Colo. 80537	Important and domestic yarns, fleeces, dyes, equipment
Lamb's End 165 W. 9 Mile Ferndale, Mich. 48220	Fibers, feathers, beads, shells, stuffing materials. Samples, $1
Lily Mills Shelby, N.C. 28150	Catalogue, $1
Naturalcraft 2199 Bancroft Way Berkeley, Calif. 94704	Yarns, cords, beads, shells, feathers. Catalogue, $1
Oldebrooke Spinnery Mountain Rd. Lebanon, N.J. 08833	Yarns, weaving and spinning supplies, books
Straw Into Gold 5509 College Ave. Berkeley, Calif. 94703	Complete fiber supplies. Dye specialists. Carry plastic ikat tape. Catalogue, $1
Yarn Depot, Inc. 545 Sutter St. San Francisco, Calif. 94102	Yarns, beads, feathers, books

Miscellaneous

Book Barn
Box 256
Avon, Conn. 06001

Crafts book specialists.
Catalogue, 50 cents

J. L. Hammett Co.
10 Hammett Pl.
Braintree, Mass. 02184

Wooden knitting rakes

Threadbare Unlimited
289 Bleecker St.
New York, N.Y. 10014

Knitting machines. Address inquiries to
Linda Mendelson

Unicorn
Box 645
Rockland, Md. 20851

Crafts book specialists.
Catalogue, $1

Index